insight text guide

Erin Geddes

The White Earth

Andrew McGahan

First published in 2020.

Insight Publications Pty Ltd
3/350 Charman Road
Cheltenham VIC 3192
Australia
Tel: +61 3 8571 4950
Fax: +61 3 8571 0257
Email: books@insightpublications.com.au

www.insightpublications.com.au

A catalogue record for this book is available from the National Library of Australia

Andrew McGahan's *The White Earth* / Erin Geddes

Erin Geddes asserts the moral right to be identified as the author of this work.

ISBNs:
9781922378033 (print)
9781922378309 (digital)
9781922378316 (bundle: print + digital)

Cover design by Gisela Beer

Printed in Australia by Ligare

contents

CHARACTER MAP

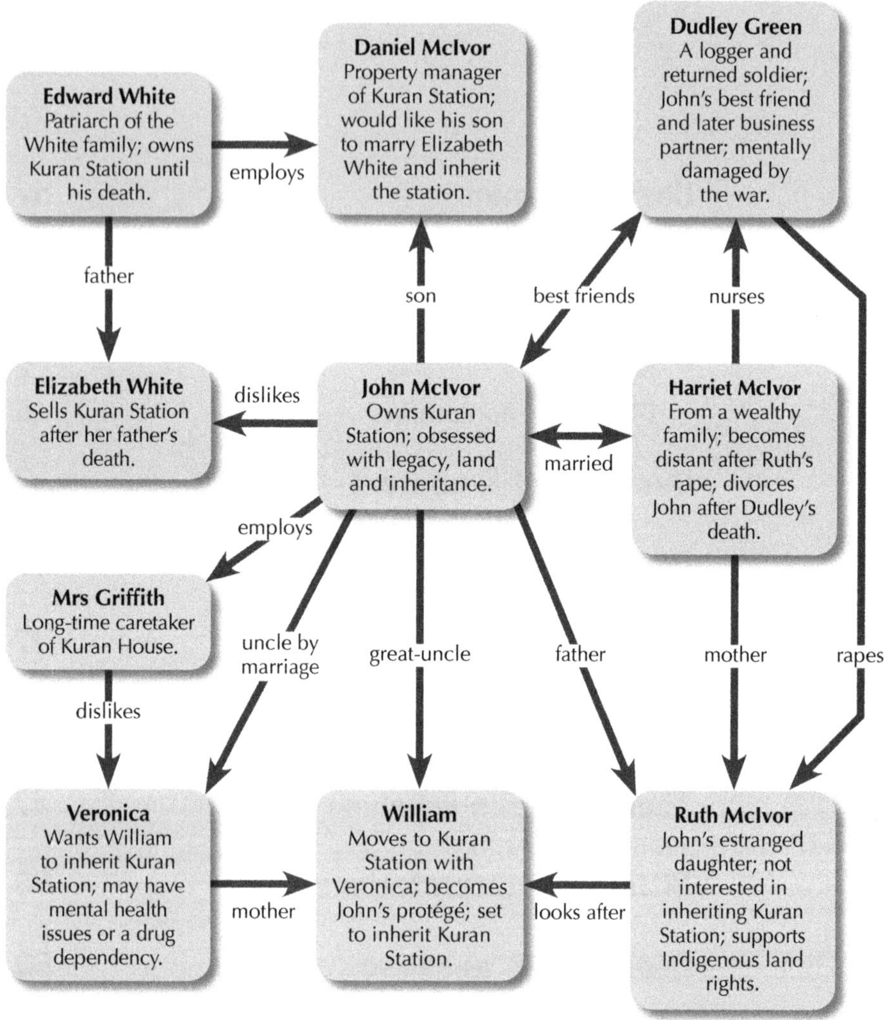

OVERVIEW

About the author

Andrew McGahan was born in Dalby, Queensland, in 1966, the son of a teacher and a farmer. He was the ninth of ten children and was educated in Dalby before finishing his senior schooling at Marist College Ashgrove in Brisbane as a boarding student. McGahan dropped out of his Arts degree at the University of Queensland to return to work on the family wheat farm. During this time he wrote his first novel, which was never published.

McGahan later moved back to Brisbane and wrote *Praise*, which won The Australian/Vogel's Literary Award for an unpublished manuscript and was published in 1991. In 1995, he revived the characters and concepts in a prequel called *1988*. McGahan wrote *Last Drinks*, *Underground* and *Wonders of a Godless World* for adults, before publishing a young adult series, Ship Kings, between 2011 and 2016. His last novel, *The Rich Man's House*, was published posthumously in September 2019. As well as writing novels, McGahan wrote the play *Bait* in 1992 and helped adapt *The White Earth* for stage. *Last Drinks* was also adapted for the stage in 2006 by Shaun Charles.

Although McGahan always maintained that *The White Earth* is a work of fiction, his agricultural background and childhood influences are obvious throughout the novel. He said in an interview with *Kill Your Darlings* magazine in 2012, 'growing up on a farm, you become really obsessed with the weather'. The weather is a critical element in *The White Earth* (see 'Genre, structure & language'), as it is in McGahan's other novels.

Andrew McGahan died in February 2019, at the age of fifty-two, from pancreatic cancer. He is considered by many to be an important Australian writer of the later twentieth and early twenty-first centuries.

Synopsis

The White Earth follows eight-year-old William. After his father dies when his harvester catches fire, William and his mother sell their farm and move in with his elderly great-uncle John (referred to in the novel as his uncle). John lives in a decrepit mansion on a property called Kuran Station in the Darling Downs, a farming region west of Brisbane. It is apparent that the housekeeper, Mrs Griffith, does not want them there, and John is reclusive during the first few weeks of their stay.

John grooms William to inherit Kuran. During their initial tour of the property, John and William encounter two visitors who are searching for sites of Aboriginal cultural significance. John denies knowledge of a waterhole but then leads William to it.

During a series of flashback chapters, the reader learns that when John was a child, his father was station manager of Kuran, then owned by a powerful farming dynasty, the White family. Daniel McIvor, John's father, has hopes of marrying John to Elizabeth White and raises John to believe that one day Kuran will be his. When Elizabeth comes of age and inherits the station, she fires Daniel and informs him of her plans to sell Kuran.

John becomes a logger in the Hoop Mountains. John and his best friend, Dudley Green, both fall in love with their employer's daughter, Harriet. When World War II starts, Dudley enlists in the army but John does not, due to both his lack of interest in the war and a logging injury that leaves him crippled in one leg. When Harriet falls pregnant to John, her father, Oliver Fisher, is enraged, but before he can act on this he dies in a bushfire in front of John. Harriet and John marry and their daughter, Ruth, is born.

In the 1993 time line, William helps his uncle prepare for a rally for the Australian Independence League, a right-wing political group run by John that opposes native title (the legal principle that recognises that Indigenous peoples have traditional rights to the land). William steals a key that enables him to explore the upper floor of Kuran House. In the study, William finds several artefacts and a military hat. Mrs Griffith discovers William and reports him to John, who explains that the artefacts belonged to a forgotten explorer who died on the property and the hat belonged to Daniel McIvor when he was in the police force. He allows William to wear the hat.

William continues to learn about John's politics in the lead-up to the rally. John is opposed to native title because of the threat it poses to pastoralists, although he is confident that changes in the law will not affect him. John continues to teach William about the land and his own deep connection to it.

The Australian Independence League committee meets and John disagrees with some members, finding their ideas too extreme. William's ear, injured by his mother earlier in the novel, causes him increasing discomfort, and he leaves the rally in pain. He has a vision of a man on fire. As he tells John, League members dressed in Ku Klux Klan robes interrupt the rally by burning wooden crucifixes.

In the earlier time line, Dudley returns from war traumatised and sick. John and Harriet care for him, and he writes John into his will as a sign of appreciation. As John's fortunes improve, he becomes obsessed with acquiring Kuran Station. John catches Dudley raping Ruth, but does not want to risk losing their inheritance by institutionalising Dudley. He sends Ruth away to boarding school so he and Harriet can continue to care for Dudley. Over the years, John acquires enough wealth to purchase Kuran, but by then Ruth has left forever.

Back in 1993, John becomes gravely ill and Mrs Griffith telephones Ruth. She arrives and learns that William might inherit Kuran. Ruth is interested in learning about William and the property in order to spite John. She opposes John on the matter of native title and tries to counteract John's influence over William.

John sends William to the waterhole to test his suitability to inherit the property. William walks for two nights and three days and sees three visions. First, he witnesses the 'jolly swagman' (a folk hero popularised by Banjo Paterson's poem 'Waltzing Matilda') violently murder another man. Second, he sees Alfred Kirchmeyer, the dead explorer whose belongings now sit in John's study. Kirchmeyer walks with William but leads him off the track. Third, he meets the terrifying bunyip, a creature that appears in Aboriginal legends, who tells him that John does not understand the real power of the property.

William makes it to the waterhole, but it is completely dry. Ruth finds him lying in the creek bed and brings him home. She tells William that Daniel McIvor was part of the Queensland Native Mounted Police and compares his hat to a Nazi uniform. She tells William and John that she has seen Malcolm White's journals that disclose information about Daniel McIvor leading a massacre of Indigenous men and boys and then covering it up by hiding the bodies in the waterhole. She explains that John could lose Kuran due to native title changes. In a rage, John insists that Dr Moffat sign his will, which names William as the inheritor of Kuran, thus making the will a legal document.

William and John visit the waterhole to collect the bones of the massacre victims. At Kuran House, John burns the bones to hide any proof of Indigenous connections to his land, but he falls into the fire, setting the whole house alight. The rest of the household escapes, but William's mother runs back into the house to find the will and is consumed by the flames. William's ear begins bleeding and he passes out.

In the epilogue, Ruth learns that the *Native Title Act 1993* has been passed by parliament and she accepts the responsibility of caring for the orphaned William.

Character summaries

William

The novel's protagonist, who is eight years old, might inherit Kuran Station if John decides to leave it to him.

John McIvor

William's great-uncle grew up on Kuran and became determined to own it and begin a new farming dynasty; he is obsessed with legacy, land and inheritance.

Veronica

William's emotionally distant mother has mental health issues and possibly a dependence on prescription drugs; she wants William to inherit Kuran for financial security.

Ruth McIvor

John's estranged daughter is a lawyer who agrees with native title reform and hates John for betraying her as a child.

Mrs Griffith

The housekeeper of Kuran House hates John and wants the house for herself; she also undermines Veronica and William whenever she can.

Doctor Moffat

John McIvor's doctor, a member of the Australian Independence League, is loyal to John, and at his request lies about William's health.

Daniel McIvor

John McIvor's father was the station manager of Kuran, and he appears in flashback chapters.

Dudley Green

John's best friend and later business partner returns from war physically and mentally damaged, and commits a terrible crime; he appears in flashback chapters.

Harriet McIvor

Harriet is in a love triangle with John and Dudley, but marries John while Dudley is fighting in World War II; she appears in flashback chapters.

Edward White

The White family patriarch, Edward owns Kuran as John grows up; he is Malcolm's father and Elizabeth's grandfather and is often manipulated by his employee Daniel McIvor; he appears in flashback chapters.

Elizabeth White

Malcolm's daughter inherits Kuran, only to sell it and fire Daniel.

BACKGROUND & CONTEXT

To understand the novel, it is important to examine critical events in Australian history, including the exposure of Indigenous massacres and the development of Indigenous civil rights in the early 1990s. *The White Earth* was published in 2004 but is set in 1993 and across several decades earlier in the twentieth century. The author references the leadership of several Australian prime ministers – Gough Whitlam, Malcolm Fraser, Bob Hawke and Paul Keating – with the benefit of hindsight due to the time between their serving and the publication of the novel.

Indigenous massacres

Many mass murders of Indigenous peoples occurred during colonial times and into the twentieth century. These massacres were euphemistically referred to as 'dispersal' of the native population.

The number of these events and the fact that they were regularly overlooked by authorities is important context for understanding the novel. Many occurred with little documentation or prosecution of perpetrators – the lack of investigation and reporting means that exact numbers, methods of killing and sometimes even the year of occurrence can be vague or lost to history. It is likely that the deaths of Indigenous peoples from frontier killings is much higher than recorded numbers suggest.

Records indicate frontier massacre victim numbers ranged from fewer than ten to over one hundred. The Mistake Creek massacre in Central Queensland resulted in an estimated 200 Indigenous deaths. Accounts report that many skulls were found on the location years later, and a station manager discussed witnessing and participating in the slaughter.

In and around the Darling Downs region, there were massacres such as Canning Creek in 1848, Yuleba Creek in 1850 and multiple clashes around the Balonne–Condamine rivers area in 1849. While it is unknown whether any of these were inspiration for the massacre mentioned in the novel, these events would have been part of McGahan's local history growing up in the area.

There were several brutal methods used to kill Indigenous peoples who resisted European colonisation. Kilcoy Station is infamous for being the location of a mass poisoning by lacing flour with arsenic and strychnine in 1842. Thirty to sixty Kabi Kabi people succumbed to poisoning, and others were shot. A poisoning of eight people took place in 1908 in Western Australia. In response to the resulting inquiry, one letter to the editor of *The West Australian* said, 'I wish to goodness Mr. Lyon Weiss [a priest who advocated for Aboriginal peoples] would let us manage our own affairs as we think best'. The notion that landowners should be allowed to 'deal with' the Indigenous presence without legal oversight is indicative of John McIvor's attitude in denying knowledge of a culturally significant waterhole on his property and, later, in retrieving and destroying the bones from the massacre.

There were very occasional examples of prosecution for the murders. Among the most famous were convictions for the Myall Creek massacre of 1838, when seven men were hanged for killing at least twenty-eight Indigenous people in northern New South Wales. Unfortunately, Myall Creek was the rare exception to the trend whereby local law enforcement would downplay or dismiss reports of massacres. Indeed, several massacres were actually initiated by law enforcement, most notably the Native Police, which consisted of groups of Indigenous men each led by a white officer.

Native title and the Mabo decision

Native title refers to the legal connection between Indigenous Australians and the land. British invasion removed Indigenous Australians' right to their traditional land. The legal basis for this was the British claiming that Australia was 'terra nullius', meaning unoccupied land. They saw it as such because Indigenous peoples did not live in dwellings or use agricultural techniques familiar to them. For more than 200 years, this was part of the legal basis for using Indigenous land, moving Indigenous peoples off their land and controlling many aspects of their lives.

Some progress towards challenging this occurred before the 1990s, most notably when the Yolngu people of the Northern Territory mounted the first Indigenous legal challenge to land rights in the 1960s. Nabalco, a mining company, acquired a lease to mine bauxite on Yolngu land. The Yolngu claimed they had been on the land since 'time immemorial' and had a continuous connection to it that would give them the right to refuse the company. Although the claim was unsuccessful, it progressed the principle of native title. In the early 1970s, the Aboriginal Land Rights Commission, a Northern Territory government inquiry, found that Indigenous peoples have rights to traditional lands and should be able to make claims to certain lands. Furthermore, it recommended that mining and tourism operators on these lands seek permission and that sacred sites be protected. Some of these recommendations would be included in the *Aboriginal Land Rights (Northern Territory) Act 1976*. And, in 1975, Prime Minister Gough Whitlam symbolically and later legally handed back land to another group of people, the Gurindji, who had famously gone on strike at Wave Hill Station because of discriminatory employment conditions and land rights.

In 1992, the legal principle of terra nullius was challenged again. The Mabo decision refers to a landmark court case. Torres Strait Islander Eddie Mabo initiated a claim that the Meriam people of Mer Island (also known as Murray Island) in the Torres Strait were the rightful owners of the land, as they had lived there according to their traditional customs and law without interruption since European colonisation. They argued in the High Court of Australia that native title was not legally extinguished by British colonisation because Indigenous peoples had lived and continue to live on traditional land. They were successful, and in June 1992 the concept of terra nullius was overturned. Eddie Mabo died in January 1992, before witnessing the verdict.

This case is important to the novel because it directly led to the *Native Title Act 1993* referred to by several characters. Prime Minister Paul Keating passed the Act, which aimed to make the decisions in the Mabo case binding law. The Act also established a process for Indigenous peoples to make claims on the land, a point Ruth reflects on in the epilogue. If Indigenous communities could prove continuous geographic and cultural connection to their land since European contact, the court could rule they may be eligible for native title, otherwise known as 'land rights'.

Post-Mabo

While *The White Earth* is set in 1993 and earlier, the author wrote the book later and thus has a different context from his characters. Native title was clarified further in 1996 with the Wik decision, which established that pastoral leases could co-exist with native title, but if there were conflicts, pastoral leases would get preference. Prime Minister John Howard led further changes through the *Native Title Amendment Act (1998)*, also known as the '10 Point Plan'. It allowed state governments to remove native title if it was in the national interest and to set time restrictions on native title claims, and outlined several other changes that allowed government control and encouraged 'co-existence' between native title claims and mining and agricultural interests.

Another important event regarding Indigenous civil rights in the 1990s was the 1997 'Bringing them Home' report. It recommended that the government apologise and offer compensation to members of the Stolen Generations – Indigenous children forcibly removed from their parents. At the time of *The White Earth*'s publication, Australia was still three years away from a formal government apology, but calls for it continued.

Although these events occurred after the time frame of the novel, they are important to understand because they make the reader aware of information the author would have had at the time of writing, and the context in which the book was published.

The Ku Klux Klan

The Ku Klux Klan is a group of right-wing extremists from the United States, easily identified by their infamous white robes and pointed white hats. Also known as The Klan or the KKK, the hate group targets black Americans, as well as immigrants, Catholics, Jews, Muslims and members of the LGBTQIA community.

The Klan had three main waves of membership. The foundation wave was in the 1860s and 1870s, in response to the abolition of slavery and the introduction of civil rights for black Americans after the American Civil War. The rituals and ceremony helped to attract members, and the Klan would become famous for lynching black Americans. In the 1920s, the second wave of Klan interest sprung from a popular silent movie, *The Birth of a Nation*. The Klan's costumes and cross-burnings drew inspiration from the film and characters in *The White Earth* use these elements on the night of the rally. From the 1950s on, the Ku Klux Klan divided into several independent branches. In 2015, the Southern Poverty Law Centre reported seventy-two active Ku Klux Klan groups, or 'chapters', in the United States.

GENRE, STRUCTURE & LANGUAGE

Genre

A notable feature of *The White Earth* is its use of the elements of Gothic horror, a genre that became popular in the nineteenth century. Ann Radcliffe's *The Mysteries of Udolpho* (1794) was one of the earliest popular examples of Gothic horror and established many features now associated with the genre. Later, writers such as Mary Shelley and Bram Stoker would continue these traditions in two of the most famous examples of Gothic horror, Shelley's *Frankenstein* (1818) and Stoker's *Dracula* (1897).

Certain settings and elements characterise Gothic horror. A motif is a repeated pattern or idea in a text. It can be used simply to build mood, or it can hold a deeper meaning. Castles, dungeons and locked rooms are classic motifs in Gothic horror, which have survived in the modern horror film. Decay and ruins, indicating old and often malevolent places and people, are also common motifs, featuring heavily in novels such as Emily Brontë's *Wuthering Heights* (1847) and Oscar Wilde's *The Picture of Dorian Gray* (1890). Instead of a castle, *The White Earth* has a decaying mansion, and there are multiple descriptions of the house as dilapidated, with 'second-storey windows that were shuttered or smashed' and the lower terrace 'littered with junk' (p.16). Staircases leading up can represent discovery or enlightenment, and in *The White Earth* William experiences this when he steals a key to explore upstairs.

Visions, hallucinations and obvious symbolism that borders on the melodramatic are other features of Gothic horror. William experiences several visions throughout the novel, including a man on fire and the three visitations when he is walking.

There are many more Gothic motifs, and further exploration of these can be helpful in understanding *The White Earth*.

Australian Gothic

Australian Gothic is a subset of the traditional Gothic horror genre. It varies in that Australia has very different landscapes and weather from Europe. This affects the colour palette that Australian authors use and results in different symbolism. Reds, browns and yellows – the colours of soil and land – feature more often than the typical blacks and greys of traditional Gothic horror.

In classic Gothic novels, bad weather is a motif often used to foreshadow doom or terrible acts. In *Dracula*, there are raging storms on the night that protagonist Jonathan Harker arrives at Dracula's castle and again when Dracula arrives in Britain. The weather is supposed to suggest something horrible will happen, building a sense of apprehension in the reader. Similarly, in Emily Brontë's *Wuthering Heights* (1847), storms parallel the characters' emotional turmoil and impending demise. Although a storm can still signal impending doom in an Australian Gothic novel, it can also signal relief from drought. Whereas summer is a welcome time in most of Europe, in Australia it can be a period of death and hardship. In *The White Earth*, the unending heat and persistent wind in the lead-up to Ruth's arrival is foreboding. During 'the scalding breath of summer' at Kuran, 'the black soil cracked open into chasms' and 'the wind thrummed and beat about the House' (p.227).

Another feature of traditional Gothic horror is the elevation of the setting to become almost a character in the story. Rather than simply being mysterious places for protagonists to enact their desires and fears, or where villains lie in wait, the rural and bush landscapes in Australian Gothic texts are often hostile, disorientating and perilous. On his journey to the waterhole, William notices that 'the surrounding hills had become unrecognisable' (p.302) and the moon 'sickly yellow, and seemed to cast no light' (p.303). Not a place of familiarity and support, William's own home rejects him and poses great danger.

A key motif in the novel is fire. William's father and Harriet's father both die in fires; William and John see the burning man; bushfires create a sense of foreboding in both the flashbacks and the 1993 time line;

and fire is used to destroy the bones of the massacre victims. Whereas fire can symbolise warmth, comfort and survival in a dreary European Gothic setting, in an Australian setting it becomes a sign of danger and destruction.

Structure

McGahan has made two particularly important structural choices in the novel. The first is the use of flashback chapters to fill in John's background and help the reader understand how he became the bitter, obsessed man he is. The literary term for flashbacks is *analepsis*, and it is used in eleven of the novel's forty-five chapters.

The flashbacks also create dramatic irony – that is, the reader has more knowledge than a character. When William explores upstairs, he finds John's room decorated with 'white curtains' and 'high white walls' (p.152), along with leather armchairs and wicker furniture. Because of the flashback, the reader understands that this room is modelled on Elizabeth White's bedroom and the impact the moment of invading her room had on John, even though William does not know these things. Similarly, when Ruth arrives in 1993, the reader understands her traumatic past and troubled relationship with her father, while William is unaware.

The second important structural choice is the use of foreshadowing, of which there are multiple instances in the novel. William's recurring ear pain, Daniel McIvor's hat and the vision of the man on fire all play important roles in the closing chapters of the novel. Possibly the most unexpected of these is the man on fire, who appears to be Oliver Fisher, but ends up being a premonition of John's own death.

Another instance of foreshadowing occurs at the beginning of Chapter 3, when the flashback time line is introduced. The opening line states that 'John McIvor's earliest memory was of smoke' (p.22). In Chapter 43, as Ruth exposes Daniel McIvor as the murderous instigator of a massacre, it becomes clear that John's earliest memory is the massacre and the burning of the bodies afterwards.

Language

A number of agricultural and legal terms are used in *The White Earth*. Most of these are explained in the key vocabulary sections of the 'Chapter-by-chapter analysis'. Several of the legal terms, such as perpetual lease land and freehold land, become increasingly important as the novel progresses.

From the title on, wordplay is present. The word 'white' in *The White Earth* could refer to the White family dynasty, the white people in the story or the irony that the land of Kuran Station is famously black soil. Additionally, 'earth' could refer to the station or the Darling Downs region in a literal sense – its soil and dirt. It can also have meaning in an abstract sense, such as the connection to land and country present in Indigenous spiritualism or that John McIvor claims to have.

Dialogue is also presented in an interesting way. In flashbacks, dialogue is in italics rather than quotation marks. This could be indicative that it is John's memory – the words are a re-telling, not necessarily the exact ones uttered. In the 1993 time line, rather than giving unimportant individual speakers names and identities, snippets of dialogue are separated by stylistic punctuation choices, such as the use of ellipsis points to separate sentence fragments on page 210:

> '… we're the ones who suffer, not the city people …'
>
> '… what do they know, they've never owned a property, worked it for generations …'

This approach conveys the fragments of conversation heard by William, drifting in and out of focus, and reflects his understanding of what is going on around him. Through these punctuation choices, the reader remains focused on what is said, rather than who is saying it.

The language reflects the Australian Gothic genre and the agricultural setting. McGahan uses imagery to depict the rural landscape and deepen characterisation, such as when William watches John: 'the flames leapt up, so that William saw his uncle as a dark shape before the fire, surrounded by ruin and rubbish, the rage rising in his voice with the flames' (p.138). Imagery such as this, rich with alliteration and evocative vocabulary, helps the reader to understand the novel's world and the people in it from William's perspective. The reader can 'see' what William sees, and experience the awe, wonder and fear that William feels.

CHAPTER-BY-CHAPTER ANALYSIS

Prologue (pp.1–4)

Summary: *William sees an explosion in the wheat fields and learns his father died in the fire that follows. He meets his uncle John.*

The prologue contains the catalyst for the novel's plot: the death of William's father, which will change the course of William's life. A wheat farm in the spring of 1992 is the setting. After the death of William senior, a man who is 'tall and grim' (p.3) comes to visit. The women fall silent at his arrival and he is introduced as 'uncle John'.

The prologue also establishes the strained relationship between William and his mother, Veronica. Even after seeing the explosion, William does not rouse Veronica, as 'he knew better than to wake her' (p.1). Later, she slaps him, 'catching his right ear in a painful, piercing smack' (p.4) for not telling her about it immediately.

Key vocabulary

Thunderhead: a type of dense, vertical cloud.

Flatbed four-wheel: a ute with a tray that has no sides so that hay and equipment can be moved easily.

Harvester: a machine that gathers crops in a harvest.

Q How does the prologue capture the spirit of a rural community?

Chapters 1–4 (pp.5–39)

Summary: *William and Veronica move into Kuran House and William begins to explore. In Chapter 3, the text moves back in time to outline John's early childhood and the history of Kuran Station.*

William moves house approximately nine months after his father dies and his world expands rapidly. Previously, his world was the house and its immediate surrounds. Beyond the yard and the shed were the silos, where he could 'see the whole farm at a glance, laid out like a quilt' (p.10). The farm and its surrounds are described in detail so that the reader understands what William is leaving.

When William first sees Kuran House, his thinks it is grand and stately, but soon notices its dilapidation: 'the gutters hung loose from the eaves, and below them, the high walls were draped in sullen vines and ivy' (p.16). This sets the mood and positions the novel as belonging to the Australian Gothic genre (see 'Genre, structure & language').

Until this point, the reader follows William's perspective. In Chapter 3, the time line changes to introduce the history of Kuran Station and John McIvor as a young man. The opening sentence, 'John McIvor's earliest memory was of smoke' (p.22), is typical of the subtle foreshadowing used throughout the book. This seemingly benign statement comes to have significance in the later tragedies in John's life that involve fire.

The original station owner began work on Kuran House, but it is the White family who finish it and establish a pastoral dynasty, being elected to the Queensland Parliament and coming to run the town of Kuran, 'a purely feudal community' (p.24). When Edward White has a granddaughter, Elizabeth, his station manager, Daniel McIvor, quickly marries and has a son, John. John McIvor grows up 'secretly believing that Kuran Station would one day be his. The thought filled him with pride' (p.27). Thus, John's sense of entitlement and the importance of inheritance is established.

In Chapter 4, the modern layout of the house, in its state of decay and neglect, is outlined. The description serves to highlight William's loneliness and isolation – instead of seeing mystery and nostalgia, he sees the ugly modifications and subdivisions, with 'no core of warmth' (p.33). The account of the house includes rich description and imagery – such as ceilings 'lost in cobwebs' and 'giant stone fireplaces' with hearths 'bricked in' and mantlepieces 'stripped away' (p.33) – that continue to establish the Gothic feel. William considers the house especially miserable at night because 'it was at night that the cold sank in deepest, as if flowing from the walls' (p.36).

Key vocabulary

Darling Downs: a farming area in southern Queensland, approximately two hours' drive west of Brisbane.

Great Dividing Range: one of the longest mountain ranges in the world, which forms a chain from Far North Queensland to western Victoria.

Chaff: the outside casing – the husk – of grains.

Squatters: originally meaning people occupying land unlawfully, in Australia the term also came to mean sheep farmers.

Selectors: farmers with crops such as wheat, who were given access to land sometimes already being used by squatters. This brought them into legal conflict.

Subdivision: a plot of land or building that has been divided into smaller sections.

Hearth: the floor of a fireplace; often referred to as the metaphorical centre of a house.

Q How is William's observation that his mother is different from the other mothers important in the characterisation of Veronica?

Key point

The introduction of flashback, or analepsis, begins to build a picture of John as a young man. It signals that John's background is crucial to the events occurring in the 1993 time line. Pay close attention to where the narrative shifts between the two time lines, and consider the effect of pausing each story at that moment.

Chapters 5–8 (pp.40–70)

Summary: *William learns he is not returning to school so that John can get to know him better. In the earlier time line, Edward White dies, and when Elizabeth returns to the property she informs Daniel and John McIvor that Kuran Station is sold, leaving the family homeless.*

In order to be exempted from school, Daniel meets Dr Moffat. In this encounter, several events that will play a part later in the novel are set in train. When Dr Moffat examines William, he irritates William's ear, which is still very sore after his mother hit him on the night of his father's death. William finds the visit confusing, as he is well, yet his mother and the doctor agree to provide the school with a medical certificate for glandular fever, revealing the sway John holds over both. Veronica asks Dr Moffat for a prescription for tryptanol, because 'it's just been too much, since the fire, with William and everything else' (p.46), perhaps indicating a drug dependency.

Chapter 6 is a flashback. John is growing up and sees himself as his father's successor at Kuran Station and its inheritor if he marries Elizabeth. Although she is not a recurring character, Elizabeth's influence is significant. After Edward White's death and his son Malcolm's tragic attempt at politics and sudden death, Elizabeth becomes the owner of Kuran. When she returns and announces to Daniel and John that the station is sold and the house will be too, she is 'unimpressed and unafraid' (p.54) in the presence of Daniel's fury. John laments his inheritance being 'ripped away' while simultaneously feeling a 'terrible admiration' (p.55) for the girl who stood up to his father, revealing a central conflict in his character between a desire for power and a fear of inadequacy.

In Chapter 7, William meets John properly for the first time when John wakes him in the middle of the night to watch a shower of shooting stars. After telling stories of strange sights, John asks William, 'did you ever see the terrible bunyip?' (p.59). John reveals that parts of the property are remote and untouched, even after years of farming, but 'you have to be able to see. Not everyone can' (p.60), indicating that he feels he has a unique and privileged connection to the property.

The next day, William begins exploring the land beyond the house and discovers a cemetery and a church, both in ruinous neglect, like the mansion.

Key vocabulary

Tryptanol: a medication used to treat depression and anxiety.

Perpetual lease: a rental contract that means the land or building can be used forever, as long as it is for the purpose stated in the contract.

Dust devils: small whirlwinds – smaller than tornadoes but powerful enough to occasionally damage property.

Bunyip: a creature in Aboriginal Australian legends that lives near creeks and billabongs and often tries to catch people who are too close to the water's edge.

Q What does Chapter 6 tell us about why John might have left the cemetery and church to decay?

Chapters 9–12 (pp.71–101)

Summary: *In the earlier time line, John's life after Kuran is difficult until he finds work as a logger in the Hoop Mountains. In 1993, John and William explore Kuran and unexpectedly meet two men on the boundary line who are interested in the property's Indigenous history.*

Chapters 9 and 12 characterise the man John will become. Through travelling the state looking for work, he comes to realise that 'the most important thing was to keep to your own country' (p.74), demonstrating again his belief in his connection to the local land.

When John sees a team of loggers carry a dying man down from the mountains, he notices 'they radiated a profound assurance in themselves' (p.76) and he decides to join them. During his time as a logger, Daniel McIvor dies, and John finds satisfaction in the mountains and a best friend in Dudley Green, a fellow logger.

John explains Kuran's history to William with pride, but his demeanour shifts when they come across a ranger and a research student camping outside Kuran's boundary. William knows that John is knowledgeable about the land and its history, but 'could sense that his uncle was being purposely uncommunicative' (p.90) when the ranger and student begin asking questions about Indigenous movement in the area and the possibility of locating a waterhole that might have 'significant finds' (p.91). After telling the men that no such waterhole exists on Kuran, John drives William to the waterhole – 'the depths were pitch black and the bottom was invisible' (p. 94) – which leaves William confused about why it must be kept secret.

Key vocabulary

Publican: someone who manages or owns a pub.

Allan Cunningham: a botanist and explorer who is credited as the first European to explore the Darling Downs and discover a way into that region through the ranges.

Mustering time: can refer to any time that livestock are assembled (mustered), but usually refers to when they are gathered for sale.

Corroborree: an important gathering in Australian Indigenous cultures that can be for sacred or non-sacred purposes, and often involves dance and storytelling.

Crown land: public land held by a state or the Commonwealth of Australia, managed by state governments; can be used for many purposes, such as airports or nature reserves.

Q How might the imagery at the end of Chapter 12 help readers understand John's feelings towards the waterhole?

Chapters 13–16 (pp.102–33)

Summary: *John continues to educate William about Kuran and John's political interest group, the Australian Independence League. In the earlier time line, John and Dudley both become involved with their boss's daughter, Harriet. John suffers a leg injury that stops his logging career and Dudley enlists to fight in World War II.*

John explains to William that his family farm was doomed to fail because William's father did not know what he was doing. John claims that sometimes people from a non-farming background 'hunger for a piece of land' (p.108) because they have never owned anything, but they do not know how to manage it.

William is hurt by the insult to his father but, after Mrs Griffith also lambasts his family, calling them 'white trash' (p.115), he decides that he does 'want the station' to be passed to him, and sees 'an image of himself as an adult, a man, moving through those golden hallways' (p.117) of Kuran, fully restored. He resolves to prove himself to his uncle.

When William begins to assist with printing the newsletter for the Australian Independence League, John reveals to him a deep mistrust of the government, his feelings on the unreliability of modern Australians and the political ambitions of his group. He also reveals that a rally of like-minded people will be taking place at Kuran in a month.

Harriet Fisher is introduced in Chapter 15. John and Dudley meet Harriet during a chance encounter and, although she has been 'born into wealth' and 'polished at respectable schools', she is 'perfectly at ease' (p.120) with them. John believes he can 'detect an emotion from Harriet that was meant uniquely for him' (p.121) yet ends up in a love triangle, with both men romantically interested in Harriet. He strikes a deal with Dudley that neither will propose to Harriet until they are both financially stable.

While John is in hospital, recovering from a logging accident that leaves his knee and shin shattered, he learns of the war. He dissuades Dudley from enlisting, but notices 'a restlessness' as Dudley 'pored over newspaper reports' (p.123) and soon cannot stop him from joining. The two men agree that neither will propose to Harriet until the war is over.

Key vocabulary

Suit: the courting or pursuing of a woman for marriage.

Dunkirk: a famous battle during World War II known for a successful evacuation of British troops.

Peter Lalor: an activist who led the Eureka Stockade, a miners' rebellion in the Ballarat goldfields in 1854.

Mr Keating: Paul Keating, Prime Minister of Australia from 1991 to 1996.

Q How would you summarise John McIvor's beliefs? Can you make connections between his past and his present?

Key point

Chapter 14 contains the moment when William decides he would like to inherit Kuran. Note that it is not during a conversation with John or in a profound flash of connection with the land. William wants Kuran after a conversation with Mrs Griffith during which she is particularly insulting about his family. Consider whether William's aspirations are noble or selfish at this point in the novel.

Chapters 17–20 (pp.134–65)

Summary: *As William continues to absorb John's world view, he sneaks into John's private rooms and discovers several artefacts. In the earlier time line, John and Harriet wait for Dudley's return, but when John sees Kuran House abandoned and decaying, his desire to own it reignites and he and Harriet consummate their relationship.*

In Chapter 17, John gets angry with William. William, who is being obedient and helpful, is confused by his rage, but soon realises that John does not want him to feel entitled to the property without earning his respect. He explains, 'I can't leave this station to someone who'll just give up when things get too hard' (p.139), demonstrating his belief that too many people do not appreciate what they have.

William steals a set of keys, which he uses to explore the upper floor. The Gothic is exemplified in the descriptions of the unaltered upstairs ceiling, 'draped with cobwebs, and whole slabs of it sagged with great, soggy bulges' (p.150). William finds John's bedroom, and is amazed to see 'white curtains that drifted in front of clear, sunlit windows' and 'high white walls that reflected the light back, so that William felt for an instant as if he was swimming in a bowl of illumination' (p.152). The reader knows – although William does not – that this was Elizabeth White's room, which John sneaked into years ago. The unchanged room shows the impact that Elizabeth had on John and is made all the more dramatic by its contrast with the rest of the house.

William finds several artefacts in a display cabinet: spectacle frames; a broken compass; a blackened fob watch, 'the face missing and the inside caked with dirt' (p.154); a leather notebook; and a single boot. He also finds a wooden trunk containing a suit, a military-style hat and a pistol. He is wearing the hat and holding the pistol when Mrs Griffith discovers him, 'her eyes blazing' (p.156).

Surprisingly, John is not mad at William, and explains that the items in the cabinet belonged to a local explorer whose biggest failure was being forgotten. He stresses to William:

> Doing something great isn't enough. Someone has to know about it, for it to mean anything. Whatever you do in this world, you have to leave someone behind who remembers. (p.163)

The theme of inheritance and legacy, at the fore of John's mind, is again emphasised.

In Chapter 20, on a particularly hot day John decides to take Harriet to a swimming place – the waterhole on Kuran. On the way, they pass the mansion. John notices that 'paint was peeling away from the verandahs, creepers were growing raggedly up the walls, and the tiles were askew on the roof' (p.144). As he drives away, his sadness and anger at the state of the house transforms into a realisation and he 'felt a sudden merging of two inner parts of himself, his childhood and his adult life, the station and the mountains ... here in this spot' (p.146). Not wanting to be 'dispossessed' of Harriet when Dudley returns, and 'afire with the joy of ownership' (p.147), he makes a move on her and they become intimate.

Key vocabulary

Dr Hewson: John Hewson, Liberal Leader of the Opposition from 1990 to 1994.

Whitlam: Gough Whitlam, Prime Minister of Australia from 1972 to 1975.

Fraser: Malcolm Fraser, Prime Minister of Australia from 1975 to 1983.

Hawke: Robert (Bob) Hawke, Prime Minister of Australia from 1983 to 1991.

AIF: the First Australian Imperial Force was the main expeditionary force of the Australian Army in World War I; Dudley volunteered for the Second Australian Imperial Force, a volunteer brigade active during World War II.

Militia: a group of civilians used to supplement the regular army in times of need (the meaning it has on p.141); can also refer to an unlawfully armed rebel group.

Guerrilla force: a small independent military group.

POWs: prisoners of war.

Q Why is legacy so important to John?

Chapters 21–4 (pp.166–97)

Summary: *In the earlier time line, John discovers Harriet is pregnant, and Oliver Fisher, Harriet's father, who opposes the union, dies in a bushfire that night. Dudley comes home from war affected physically and mentally, and signs his property over to John for his assistance and care. In 1993, John and William prepare for the rally.*

Chapter 21 has a particularly important recurring motif: fire. When Oliver Fisher dies in the bushfire before he can take steps to ensure John and Harriet will not be together, the last thing John sees of Oliver is 'a flailing, burning shape of arms and legs' (p.170). Just as it features in William's father's death and will feature again, fire becomes both an obstacle and a means for overcoming problems.

Several important events follow from Oliver's death. When John learns the fire that killed Oliver began on Kuran Station, he believes that 'the hills of his station had ignited by themselves that night, and so devoured his enemy' (p.171). John's sense of destiny and entitlement, reignited in the previous chapter, is again in full force. Oliver's fortune is smaller than expected, and after the war the sawmill is sold, meaning 'Oliver's legacy was complete' (p.171). John wishes for a longer-lasting legacy for himself. John and Harriet marry, buy a small farm and give birth to a daughter, Ruth.

Dudley returns from war a changed man. After his parents die, John and Harriet ensure that Dudley is looked after and that his farm is tended. Unexpectedly, Dudley signs his power of attorney over to John, and leaves his property to John in his will.

In the lead-up to the rally, William learns from television that there are other perspectives on native title besides his uncle's. John continues to share his opinion with William: he believes it is 'far too late to undo the things that were done' (p.180) and that he must fight native title legislation so that he and others do not feel the need to hide the existence of culturally significant Indigenous sites. John believes he has a connection with the land as deep or significant as any Indigenous person – 'this land talks to me' (p.181) – and does not see himself or the League as racist, but warns William that racist people will be attending the rally.

Once the committee members arrive at Kuran Station, they vote for a militia arm of the League, despite John's hesitations. Although he is president, it becomes apparent that he has less control than he would like.

Key vocabulary

Bora rings: circular Indigenous ceremonial grounds with raised earth or stones around the perimeter.

Freehold: ownership of a property or building.

Leasehold: the right to use a property for the time specified in a contract.

Dysentery: an infectious disease that affects the bowels.

Beriberi: a disease that causes pain and paralysis in the extremities, caused by a deficiency of vitamin B1.

Malaria: a tropical disease spread by mosquitoes, causing fever.

Q What does fire symbolise, and why might McGahan use it to signify important events in the novel?

Chapters 25–8 (pp.198–232)

Summary: *William's ear pain causes him to leave the rally, and he sees a man on fire moving through the trees. People in white robes burning wooden crosses ruin the rally. John becomes gravely ill and Mrs Griffith telephones Ruth. In the earlier time line, Dudley rapes twelve-year-old Ruth. Rather than risk losing Dudley's property, John convinces Harriet to send Ruth to boarding school.*

These chapters cover critical changes in both time lines. The rally is described from William's perspective in detail rich with imagery. He does not question proceedings until 'Waltzing Matilda' is sung instead of the Australian national anthem. John explains that the song's 'point was that the little man had had enough' (p.203) and that this reflects the feelings of the League members.

In the evening, William's ear pain becomes intense. He runs off only to realise that he can see the same flame he saw in the hills after his father died. Up close, he sees it is a man on fire, the flames 'utterly without sound' (p.214), standing motionless. He is terrified of his vision and runs back to the rally to tell John, only to realise that actual fire is 'rushing up over the brow of a hill' (p.216) as a giant wooden cross comes into view, carried by men in white robes, and John protests 'this isn't the Australian way. This is from somewhere else' (p.216). The 'somewhere else' is America, home of the Ku Klux Klan (see 'Background & context').

After the rally, Veronica is worried that John will die before signing Kuran over to William. She takes over the care of John from Mrs Griffith. Mrs Griffith triumphantly announces that she has telephoned Ruth, who is coming.

In Chapter 27, it is 1956 and John realises he has never told Harriet about his plan to purchase Kuran. After Dudley rapes Ruth, John is worried that 'the path he had laid out for himself and his family, leading all the way to the front door of Kuran House' (p.222) could be ruined. A gulf emerges between himself and Harriet, as she begins to see John as not simply determined but 'cold and calculating' (p.223), yet they agree to send Ruth to boarding school so they can continue to care for Dudley.

Key vocabulary

Billycan: a metal bucket used over a fire for making tea and cooking food.

Holden Commodore: an iconic Australian car.

Q In what ways are the rally and Ruth's rape turning points for each time line?

Q Consider the role that control plays in John's life.

Key point

The rally reveals several things about John's character that William does not understand straight away. It shows that although he is president of the Australian Independence League, he does not have as much sway over it as he would like. Despite often doing what he wants without regard for others, John feels betrayed that members of the League would do something he disapproves of without telling him.

Chapters 29–32 (pp.233–64)

Summary: *William sees John for the first time since the rally. Ruth arrives and speaks with William about Kuran. In the earlier time line, Harriet's withdrawal from society and from John, and Ruth's growth and wilful nature, are explored.*

John asks to see William to discuss the events at the rally and William's vision of a man on fire. The reader knows that John has seen and dreamt about a burning man, but when William asks about this, John 'only smiled, closed his eyes' (p.241).

Ruth's arrival sharpens tensions at Kuran Station. The assumption that William will inherit the station becomes obvious when John makes Ruth ask William if she may stay on the property. William learns it is not simply money that has hindered the restoration of Kuran House: Ruth reveals that ten years ago the Heritage Trust was interested in restoring the dwelling and 'all they needed was my father's permission' (p.259). When Harriet left John, the poor condition of the house became a badge of John's hardship, to 'show everyone how badly the world has treated him' (p.261), Ruth believes.

Chapter 30 focuses on the influence Brisbane and university has on Ruth and the increasing resentment and isolation of Harriet. Although still told from John's perspective, the chapter gives insight into these two women whose lives are so influenced by his choices. Harriet, nursing Dudley on his deathbed, 'wished she had never met either Dudley *or* John' (p.244). She withdraws from community work and other interests until she is housebound. Meanwhile, Ruth becomes more 'alien' (p.246) to her father – he cannot understand why she would wear or say or think the things she does.

After Dudley's death in 1968, John inherits Dudley's farm, but his reputation in the community diminishes even further. The distance between John and Ruth becomes more 'unbridgeable' (p.247) until, one day the following year, Ruth comes home with a husband in tow.

Key vocabulary

Fascists: people who adhere to fascism, an authoritarian belief system that focuses on the nation above the individual and advocates forceful oppression of dissent.

Q How is John's belief in inheritance and legacy reinforced and challenged in these chapters?

Chapters 33–6 (pp.265–97)

Summary: *In the earlier time line, Ruth visits Kuran for what she believes is the last time. In 1993, William realises Ruth is manipulating him. He accidentally reveals that the farm is a perpetual lease. John tells William he must go to the waterhole.*

John cuts Ruth off emotionally and financially after her visit home with her husband, Carl, 'a confirmed anarchist' and 'the son of two university lecturers' (p.267). John wishes for Kuran to become 'the foundation of a new dynasty, eclipsing even the Whites' (p.267), but he knows that the distance between himself and Ruth means she will not understand his plans. Rather than being upset at being cut off, Ruth displays 'a triumphant, shining anger' (p.270), and John realises he is alone now in his ambitions.

Key point

The rift between Ruth and John is revealed as irreparable. Ruth will never forgive John for sending her away after the sexual assault, and John will never understand why Ruth wants to be with someone like Carl and live the lifestyle she does.

In 1993, the reader becomes familiar with Ruth's character. She is intelligent and calculating, and knows how to manipulate William to get the information she seeks. Although she has very different goals and values from John, the similarities to her father are clear.

Ruth knows about the house's history and the White family, but argues that John has become like Edward White, 'another old man, clinging on to this bloody station for dear life' (p.279). Even though William is aware that Ruth is trying to undermine his trust and belief in John, he discloses that the farm is a perpetual lease, which interests Ruth. John asks her to leave Kuran, which she does, but not before warning William, 'my father won't give you this place for free ... be careful of what he tells you to do' (p.288).

John chastises William for giving information to Ruth, dismissing her 'clever lies' (p.292), but shares that he has once had a vision at the waterhole where the land spoke to him. He insists that the land 'wants' (p.296) William too and he must go to the waterhole, alone, at once.

Key vocabulary

Anarchist: someone who follows anarchism, a radical political movement that rejects authority.

Libertarian socialism: an anti-capitalist movement that would see wealth redistributed to all people and distrusts government interference.

Cherbourg: a large reserve in south-east Queensland that housed Indigenous people during the twentieth century. The government displaced many Indigenous people from their own lands in Queensland and moved them to Cherbourg.

Q How does Ruth challenge William's world view? What themes in the novel do these challenges connect to?

Chapters 37–40 (pp.298–328)

Summary: *While travelling to the waterhole, William has three visions. After being rescued by Ruth, he realises his mother will never really be able to care for him.*

William begins his journey, but it quickly deteriorates due to heat and lack of water. These chapters mark a full immersion into a journey of discovery and insight, an element sometimes seen in the Gothic horror genre.

William walks for nearly three days and has three visions. First, he sees a man dragging someone along then killing them with an axe. William watches as 'the axeman laughed, and brought the weapon down again. And again' (p.304). William does not know it, but he is having a vision of the 'jolly swagman' sung about at the rally. The swagman wants to hurt William too, but stops when he realises William is wearing the old police hat that belonged to Daniel McIvor.

Next, William sees Alfred Kirchmeyer, who travels with him and will not leave him alone – 'then he would open his eyes again, and the ragged figure would be there beside him' (p.311) – even though he knows this is a hallucination. When William finally wakes 'from his long stupor' (p.312), he realises that he has walked in the wrong direction, off the track, and is alone in the bush.

William eventually finds himself at 'the foot of a low hill' (p.315) and he meets the bunyip, whose 'enormous head was tilted to the night sky … when the creature shifted on its slow haunches, it became a multitude of shapes, and no shape at all' (pp.315–16). The bunyip reveals that John is 'blind' to the landscape's cultural significance but William bears 'the mark' (p.317). He tells William, 'the dead are ready for you now' (p.317).

William eventually finds the waterhole and is devastated to find it is completely dry, which is rarely the case. After Ruth finds him and brings him back to the house, William realises his mother is too weak to stand up to John, 'and the last remnant of faith he had in her died' (p.325).

Q What effect is achieved by presenting each of the three visions in their own chapter? Consider the narrative momentum and pace, as well as the description of each vision and the insights they provide to William on his journey.

Key point

The visions occur in a way common to such stories. William has three separate visions, as three is an important number to many cultures around the world. Each vision is a mixture of the familiar and the feared: the swagman, the explorer and the bunyip are all stories that John has shared with William, but they are mixed with things William is afraid of – death, getting lost and the truth. Finally, each vision leads William to a new insight, leaving him wiser and equipped with the knowledge he needs, but not necessarily happier.

Chapters 41–5 (pp.329–70)

Summary: *Ruth reveals to John and William that Daniel McIvor was responsible for an Indigenous massacre. John signs Kuran over to William in front of her. After William tells John about the bones in the creek bed, they gather the bones and start a fire to destroy them. John falls into the fire and burns to death, setting the house alight. Ruth, Mrs Griffith and William escape, but Veronica runs back for the will.*

The final chapters reveal all secrets and deceptions to the characters and the reader. Considering the significance of secrets and mysteries to the story, these elements need to be resolved in order for the narrative to come to a satisfying close.

Ruth tells William that Daniel McIvor was part of the Queensland Native Mounted Police, who killed many Indigenous people before Edward White employed him. It is why she finds the police hat disgusting, because it meant William was 'dressed up in the Australian equivalent of an SS uniform' (p.336).

Producing Malcolm White's journals, Ruth confronts John about Daniel McIvor's leadership of a massacre of Indigenous men and boys at the waterhole. No-one reported it because 'his own men were terrified of him', but it made him an 'outcast' (p.349). Ruth believes this proves the descendants of these men, whom she met at Cherbourg, could launch a native title claim. In 'unveiled loathing' (p.355) John signs Kuran over to William in front of Ruth, goading her afterwards, 'so go ahead and help your friends with their claim. It won't be me you're hurting' (p.357).

Later, William confesses that he saw bones in the dry waterhole: 'the things out in the hills. They said I'd find it!' (p.359). In one last attempt at secrecy, John takes William to the waterhole before the rain arrives, and William collects the bones in order to remove proof of the massacre and the Indigenous people's connection with the land. William disassociates himself from his actions 'as his hands picked at the bones' (p.364).

John lights a fire to burn the bones, but his bad knee gives way and sends him into the flames, with 'burning wood and bones scattering everywhere' (p.366). Despite her hatred of her father, Ruth tries to save him, but it is too late: 'a burning shape walked through the door. It was wrapped in smoke and flame' (p.367).

The rest of the household escapes safely, but William sees his mother 'heading back towards the House' (p.368) and realises it is because she wants to retrieve John's will, which names William as the owner of Kuran. Before she can re-emerge, the house 'dies', making 'a long anguished sound … and then, with slow majesty, the blazing line of the roof began to sag inwards' (p.369). William is left injured and his ear begins to bleed. He lies down on 'the cool earth' (p.370) and loses consciousness.

Key vocabulary

SS: short for Schutzstaffel, Adolf Hitler's special police in Nazi Germany.

Q What are all the possible meanings of the title of the novel?

Epilogue (pp.371–6)

Summary: *Ruth reads about the passing of native title legislation in the paper while she is at William's hospital bedside. She realises he has no-one else to look after him.*

The epilogue offers an ambiguous resolution to the story of Kuran Station: just as it is not the end of the native title debate in Australia, the property is not immune from claim, and the future is uncertain. Ruth realises how much like her father she is when she decides that the Indigenous women who might make a native title claim to Kuran would have to go through the legal process, even though it might be in her power to simply grant them the land, because 'in this world, something like that wasn't just given back. It had to be fought for' (p.375).

The last pages also reveal the final mystery in William's story: his ear was making him very sick, but in his neglect and others' greed, no-one noticed. The reader knows that his future lies with Ruth – although she moves towards the door to leave, Ruth returns to his bedside for 'the long vigil of the night' (p.376).

Q What arguments could be made for and against the idea that this is a coming-of-age story?

CHARACTERS & RELATIONSHIPS

John McIvor

Key quotes

'No one is taking one square inch of my land away. I've kept this station alive despite everything the world has thrown at me. And I did it alone.' (p.139)

'... there was no sign of weakness in his eyes, no acceptance of defeat, only the madness burning.' (p. 362)

John is undoubtedly the most complex and domineering character in *The White Earth*. The flashbacks provide detailed insight into key events that shape him into the old man of the 1993 time line. From an early age, a sense of entitlement is instilled in him and he believes he is worthy and destined to own Kuran Station.

John McIvor is the son of Daniel McIvor, the influential station manager at Kuran and a former member of the Queensland Police. Near the end of the novel, Ruth reveals that Daniel was actually an officer in the Queensland Native Mounted Police, created to control Indigenous groups around Queensland (see 'Background & context'). John's initial childhood memories in Chapter 3 become foreshadowing for the massacre he unwittingly witnessed as a child. Until this revelation near the end of the novel, the descriptions of his childhood appear only to characterise Daniel's and John's growing sense of inevitable ownership of Kuran.

It is not until John leaves Kuran and becomes a logger that he stops regarding 'land purely as an inanimate thing' (p.100). His time in the mountains forges his friendship with Dudley Green and shapes his connection with the land. He wonders about certain places in the mountains that 'spoke to man' (p.99) and contained secrets. He sees himself as one of the few people who can access the secrets of the land, but later, ironically, he wants to deny Indigenous people the ability to access those secrets. He thinks that Indigenous people 'were gone and wouldn't be coming back' (p.100). John's actions undermine any respect for Indigenous people he claims to have.

John's possessiveness pervades many events in the novel and consistently drives his actions. Chapter 18 shows John 'claiming' Harriet at the waterhole, despite his arrangement with Dudley to wait. In his first outing with John, William 'could hear the pride in the way his uncle said "my land"' (p.82). John explains to William 'the shire council or the government or someone else might try to take the water hole away from us' (p.103). Although he acknowledges that someone will inevitably inherit the land and he would like it to be William, John insists, even as he and William are violating graves in the middle of the night to hide evidence, 'they must never take this land from me' (p.364). In reality, John would like to have inherited Kuran as a young man the way he 'should' have.

John is a contradictory character. His flashback chapters show him having little consideration for his mother, father and sister. He begins his own journey into fatherhood positively but values the possibility of purchasing Kuran over the care and nurture of Ruth. He neglects his wife until 'her sorrows were an irrelevance to him' (p.246). Despite this disregard for his immediate family, he chooses William, a distant relative, as the future inheritor of Kuran and invests a great deal of time and energy in mentoring him.

John's ownership of Kuran gives him power over almost every other character. It is the desire for Kuran that allows Veronica, Mrs Griffith and, to a lesser extent, William to be manipulated by John. For a time, William evokes a fatherly side to John, and John, with the benefit of hindsight, does not repeat the mistake of failing to communicate his ambitions to his family: he shares his opinions, beliefs and politics with William. When explaining to William why the Australian Independence League he set up sings 'Waltzing Matilda' instead of the national anthem, he says that the swagman appeals because 'the little man had had enough' (p.203) and 'Waltzing Matilda' is a cautionary tale for Australia 'if we don't watch out' (p.204).

In the end, John's hatred of native title, coupled with his own paranoia and possessiveness, proves to be his downfall. His obsession with creating a legacy to pass on causes him to behave irrationally and desecrate the graves at the waterhole. It is ironic that while burning these remains, his knee injury, which led him to Harriet's arms and Kuran's door, causes his leg to give way and results in his death.

Key point

Not all characters have to be consistently likeable to be well drawn or to add meaning to a text. John exemplifies this. His actions at the end of the novel are reprehensible, but at early points he is a sympathetic character. Consider whether any of the adults in the novel are completely likeable, or even whether William is.

William

Key quotes

'It had never occurred to him to be proud of his little farm back home. How could you be proud of a square mile of dirt?' (p.82)

'He'd been doing his best, to help, to grow up. What had he done that was so wrong?' (p.139)

William is the protagonist of *The White Earth* – the novel follows him and the reader sees the events of the 1993 time line through his perspective. In the prologue, he seems a quiet, passive character who knows better than to wake his mother to tell her about the explosion in the field. After his father's death, he observes the comings and goings of visitors with little emotion and thinks that 'perhaps he had a right to be angry at his father' (p.6) for leaving him and his mother in financial instability, but ultimately he is not. His relationship with his mother is not as benign: 'his feelings about her had always been more complex' (p.7).

William is charactised as lonely and isolated at first. Despite William being absent from school for six months, no-one outside Kuran shows any particular concern for him: no telephone call or letter arrives from any friend or teacher. On the day of the rally, he 'trailed the other kids' (p.200) but has no conversations and makes no friends. McGahan never states William and Veronica's surname in the novel. This reinforces that William has inherited little from his father. With no legacy, no family history, bestowed on him, he is a blank, obedient slate on which John can inscribe his own views and values.

William's most important relationship in the novel is with John. It is William's ability to 'see' visions in the world around him that bonds him to John. At the rally, William has a vivid vision of a man on fire. This is the same vision that John has seen all his adult life. John takes this as a sign that William might be worthy of inheriting Kuran Station. The bunyip tells William 'you bear the mark, boy' (p.317) and William realises it means the badge on his captain's hat. The badge also saves William from the swagman in an earlier vision because the swagman recognises it as a sign of authority. After the bunyip reveals that John is mistaken about the power of the stone circle on the hill – 'the old man is blind' (p.317) – William tells John 'the things out in the hills. They said I'd find it!' (p.359), realising that the bunyip is right, and that John has a 'blindness' to the secrets of the land.

John teaches William that a farm is not simply the soil, but a connected, living entity to be understood and respected. He also influences William to feel opposed to native title legislation. But the most important change John instigates in William is a desire to own Kuran. It is the first real aspiration William has in the novel. He pictures himself as an adult in the grandly restored halls of Kuran and 'in that moment, he made up his mind. He *did* want the station' (p.117).

Despite this ambition, William remains childlike and innocent for much of the novel. He is enthusiastic for the political rally on John's property because 'maybe he would get to sleep in a tent' (p.132). After the rally, he wonders 'where had those three committee members been when the white-hooded men appeared?' (p.230) and even though he has suspicions, he still needs John to confirm that the committee members were also the Klan members.

Even towards the end of the novel, William is still somewhat naive and trusting. When Ruth tries to open his mind to other ways of interpreting native title and William becomes defensive, Ruth says 'that's your uncle talking' (p.284). William's loyalty to John extends so far that he tells John about the bones in the waterhole, and helps him to desecrate the graves of the massacre victims. This experience could be seen to bring him from innocence to experience, so that the William in the hospital bed at the novel's end is wiser and more alert than the boy who moved to Kuran.

Ruth

Key quotes

'... her father, whom she had always adored, had not only failed to save her that night, but had now convinced her mother to send her away.' (p.224)

'She'll pretend to be your friend ...' (John, p.241)

It is through the flashbacks that readers come to understand Ruth and her motivation to return to Kuran before she even arrives in the 1993 time line. As a child, Ruth has a close relationship with her parents, John and Harriet, but she never recovers from the betrayal she feels when John sends her to boarding school after Dudley rapes her. Their relationship becomes transactional: Ruth makes decisions without her parents' input and then 'demanded their financial support' (p.243).

Although John wants Kuran Station as a family farm for Ruth to inherit, younger Ruth is unaware of 'the whole life he'd always planned for her' (p.267). At university, she becomes open to new ideas, politics and lifestyles. It is not clear from John's perspective whether some of these choices are made to spite him. Ruth arriving with a husband she knows her father will hate is seemingly part of the spite directed towards him. John believes Ruth has sex with her husband in his house as an act of revenge for her rape. His anger and disappointment with her are evident, but just as Elizabeth White is beyond caring about Daniel McIvor's rage, so too is Ruth indifferent to John's censure.

As an adult, Ruth is the only person who tries to understand William. Whereas John tests William to ensure he has absorbed John's wisdom, Ruth enters into dialogue with William to challenge his notions of ownership, land and native title. Like most of the adults in William's life, Ruth wants something from him – in her case, information – but she also shows empathy for William. Although she manipulates him to confess that Kuran Station is a perpetual lease, not freehold land, she also rescues him from the bush when he journeys to the waterhole. Of the adults surrounding him, Ruth alone seems to understand that William is only a child and that John is asking a lot of him. She tells William: 'this inheritance business is for his sake, not yours' (p.279). Ruth calls John 'another old man, clinging on to this bloody station for dear life' (p.279) and teaches William that 'other people were already here' (p.276) in Darling Downs – it wasn't empty when it was 'discovered' by European explorers – which confuses William and challenges the beliefs he has learnt from John.

Ruth performs several critical actions in the novel. First, her decision to return to Kuran disrupts the plan that Veronica has for William to inherit the station without opposition. Second, Ruth rescues William after his journey to the waterhole, not hesitating to search for him when his own mother hesitates. Afterwards she reminds William that he doesn't 'have to do anything' John says, 'not after what he's done' (p.331). Third, Ruth researches Daniel McIvor. She discovers that he led a massacre at the waterhole and that the victims' descendants could make a claim to Kuran should the native title legislation pass. Although she clearly aims to disrupt her father's plans in whatever way she can, Ruth's redeeming feature is her care for William, which is shown to be unconditional, if reluctantly given, in the epilogue.

Veronica

Key quotes

'Has he written anything down on paper about you? Because if he hasn't, then what's the point of any of this?' (p.226)

'The thing is, people like your parents, sometimes they hunger for a piece of land, because they've never had anything of their own before …' (John to William, pp.108–9)

Veronica's mental health is a key factor in her personality. In Chapter 1, her history of headaches, exhaustion and anger leads to her screaming and slapping William. Veronica takes 'many pills', visits the doctor often and on several occasions goes away to 'a place where people went when they needed time away by themselves' (p.7). When she meets Doctor Moffat, she asks for tryptanol, a medication for depression and anxiety, but she does not fill the prescription until later in the novel. Whether she suffers from mental illness, drug dependency or both remains ambiguous.

Veronica's greed is emphasised throughout the novel. Both Mrs Griffith and John accuse Veronica of wanting to own Kuran. When William questions why they have moved to the station, she responds, 'there are things you don't understand, and I don't want you ruining them' (p.38). She agrees to William missing six months of school so that John can come to know him, in the hope that John will name him his sole beneficiary; she tells William, 'you'll have to grow up fast. You have to do this for me' (p.113).

Veronica and William have an atypical mother–son relationship. She drifts in and out of his focus, making little impact on his life at Kuran. Veronica appears to be a poor mother who has little influence on William's life: conversations she has with William do not have significant effect on his actions. There are several instances where Veronica seems concerned for William but he soon realises it is about Kuran. One example is after the rally, when William perceives that Veronica is upset not 'because her son had been sick' (p.226) but because John could have died before signing Kuran over to William. This revelation causes

William to feel a 'coldness' (p.226) inside him. He gradually loses his connection to his mother. He understands that when Veronica takes over the care of John after his heart attack, it is because 'she was trying to secure their place his heart' (p.229). Veronica's determination to inherit Kuran shows that she is focused and calculating.

William is furious with his mother after Ruth rescues him from the waterhole, and Veronica admits 'it should have been me that found you' (p.324). For a moment it appears they might reconcile, and William takes the chance to ask about treatment for his ear. However, Veronica's response that William can only visit the doctor once his bruises disappear kills 'the last remnant of faith' (p.325) he has in her. William knows that this is to avoid accusations of child neglect. This scene severs the bond William has with his mother, so when she runs into the fire to retrieve John's will, the reader knows that William will not take too long to accept her fate.

Mrs Griffith

Key quotes

'Now that his uncle was gone, the housekeeper patrolled the hallways with a special vigilance, wrapped in her cardigans.' (p.114)

'... later that night, when William and his mother sat down for dinner, the housekeeper was back, rocking with some secret pleasure at her end of the table.' (p.231)

Mrs Griffith, the housekeeper at Kuran House, serves several purposes in the novel. For one, she lays bare Veronica's greed. Her actions and words to William are full of blunt venom. She ensures that William knows about Veronica's troubled childhood and calls her 'a dirty little thing' and 'a little touched' (p.115). Despite this, she is also the person who helps William realise that he wants to inherit Kuran for himself, not just because his mother told him to.

Mrs Griffith also acts as a hindrance to Veronica and William in their quest to inherit Kuran. She catches William in the red room and he understands 'she'd been waiting all along for him to make a mistake' (p.158). After her attempt to disgrace William backfires, she seems 'bereft' and 'diminished' (p.229), 'glancing always towards the ceiling' (p.231), towards John's bedroom. In keeping with Gothic motif, Mrs Griffith becomes akin to a phantom or a ghost – she is the living spectre who haunts the house. Nonetheless, she telephones Ruth as a last bid to stop William from inheriting Kuran.

Like John, Mrs Griffith has a long connection to the property and a sense of ownership of and entitlement to the house. She has lived and worked on the station since she was a child. John tells William 'she was furious when I moved in' (p.61) but does not fire her because he needs someone to cook, clean and do laundry. In the epilogue, Ruth reflects that Mrs Griffith has 'lost none of her grim tenacity' (p.375) and is demanding compensation for lack of payment from John. The reader knows that, even after the novel's close, Mrs Griffith will continue to be a nuisance to William and Ruth.

Harriet McIvor

Key quotes

' ... there was a side to her that appreciated the gravity in John, and which shared, in part, his wariness of the world.' (p.121)

'There were moments ... when she wished she had never met either Dudley *or* John.' (p.244)

Apart from her 'education and grace' (p.120), the reader learns little of Harriet until later in the novel. Initially, she serves as the object of John's and Dudley's desires. John believes he can 'detect an emotion from Harriet ... meant uniquely for him' (p.121). She appears passive but willing when John makes a sexual advance at the waterhole, and her reaction to marrying him is not shown. Most of her strong feelings emerge after Ruth is sent to boarding school. Harriet resents that Dudley, the man who raped Ruth, has 'chained her to this sickroom' and is dying 'right in front of her, so slowly, in her own house' (p.244). Her emotions towards Dudley are more complex than simple hate: she also pities him for the damage he has suffered from the war. She resents John for making decisions without regard for her and for the humiliation she experiences in town when neighbours gossip about their relationship with Dudley. Harriet becomes 'the strange, reclusive wife of an even stranger man' (p.246), and after Dudley's death she divorces John, making him even more bitter than he already was.

Dudley Green

Key quote

> 'The camps had leached the brightness out of him, broken something inside.' (p.193)

Dudley is a man of dualities. He begins as a cheerful, talkative contrast to John and later becomes his romantic rival. His personality creates a character foil for John. He is a sympathetic listener when John wants to discuss his past. As young men they make plans to go into business together, although this does not eventuate in the way they hope. Dudley enlists to fight in World War II, and returns 'a forlorn shadow' (p.193) of his former self. He has both physical and mental issues following the war. He never discusses whether he is upset about John marrying Harriet while he was away and is happy to be an uncle figure to Ruth. He is so grateful to John and Harriet for looking after him following the death of his parents that he changes his will so that John inherits his farm.

After Dudley rapes Ruth, he makes no more decisions that affect the outcome of the novel. Rather, John and Harriet make choices for him. Dudley does not seem aware that John's kindness is based on ensuring he inherits Dudley's farm. Harriet grows to resent having to care for Dudley, knowing 'full well that he should be in hospital' (p.244). When Dudley dies a pitiable character, John fights for and wins possession of his estate.

Doctor Moffat

Key quote

'The man smelled of old clothes and alcohol, and his puffy eyes were etched with red.' (p.41)

Doctor Moffat is a weak-willed character, under the sway of John. When he is introduced in Chapter 5, the reader learns he is John's doctor and also a member of the Australian Independence League's committee. One of the first things he does is agree to commit fraud for John by writing a fake medical certificate for William. He does not notice that the boy's ear is causing him intense pain, even when William draws attention to it. Later in the novel, when William questions whether Doctor Moffat is a good doctor, Veronica admits, 'no, I don't suppose he is' (p.325).

Doctor Moffat's purpose in the story is more than being an inadequate doctor. His role is to legitimise the choices that John and Veronica make about William and to keep them secret. His involvement makes William's fraudulent absence from school seem legitimate to the authorities. Later, when William is injured, first at the rally and then during his journey to the waterhole, he is examined by Doctor Moffat. In other circumstances, William's injuries might have resulted in a visit to a town doctor or hospital. Doctor Moffat's presence means that, to William, Kuran remains all-encompassing, sealed off from the wider world. In the epilogue, William's physical condition is severe enough that the hospital staff 'would have referred the case to a social worker, on the suspicion of parental neglect' (p.374) if Veronica had lived.

Key point

Minor characters in *The White Earth* are not always as well developed as main characters, but they play an important role. The character of Harriet is given more focus in the novel than Doctor Moffat or Dudley, yet both of these characters' actions arguably have more impact on the events of the story.

THEMES, IDEAS & VALUES

Greed and entitlement

Key quotes

'I should've had this property sixty years ago. Instead I had to fight my whole life to get it.' (John, p.137)

'Now she's gone and found another man, hasn't she, with a big House, up on a hill.' (Mrs Griffith about Veronica, p.116)

Greed and entitlement are critical themes in *The White Earth*. When Elizabeth White is born, Daniel McIvor quickly has a son, whom he hopes could marry Elizabeth. John grows up 'secretly believing that Kuran Station would one day be his. The thought filled him with pride' (p.27). The expectation of owning Kuran is what drives John. As his fortunes grow, he feels more entitled to Kuran, and what begins as aspiration becomes bloody-mindedness. Eventually, his sense of entitlement becomes a sense of destiny. He sees his connection with the land as a sign that he is its true and rightful owner. When Oliver Fisher dies in a bushfire and John learns it began on Kuran, he believes that the land 'devoured his enemy' (p.171) for him.

It is not that John does not work hard over the course of his life. As a farmer with a young family, he researches, plans and fails many times. There are bad years of crops. A talent for farming and hard work help him to overcome difficult times. But his manipulation and then forgiveness of Dudley, which could certainly be classified as motivated by greed, also plays a significant role. He craves the wealth to buy Kuran and will stop at nothing to get it.

Eventually, John's greed turns to fear. He has all he ever wanted except a clear heir, and he fears that his efforts to secure Kuran will be pointless. Even William finally sees this. Although it is William who tells John about the bones, in the moment before they begin to collect them he realises that John is 'hollow and wretched and beyond hope' (p.364) and that owning Kuran has not brought him happiness.

Whereas John feels some kind of divine entitlement to Kuran, Veronica is motivated only by greed and fear. She sees in Kuran a means to financial security. After William's father dies, she asks William frantically, 'where's the money going to come from?' (p.38) and later, when John has told William he might leave Kuran to him, Veronica confides in her son, 'this property is worth a lot of money – we could sell it and move away to somewhere nice' (p.113). This supports John's belief that people without land 'think a few hundred acres will make all the difference' (p.109) but they don't value the land enough to appreciate it.

Veronica's greed leads directly to her death. In the closing chapter, she rushes back into the burning house for John's will, because 'all she had ever wanted' is 'contained in that one piece of paper' (p.369).

As a maid working at Kuran House in her youth, Mrs Griffith would have been given no promises like those Daniel McIvor made to his son, yet she feels that the station is her home and is bent on claiming it. Her initial strategy to stake her claim is simply refusing to leave. John shares some of Mrs Griffith's background with William, telling him that 'managers have come and gone, but not her'. He believes she has 'sworn to outlive me, just so she'll be alone here again' (p.61). Once William and Veronica arrive, it is 'plain that the housekeeper considered them unwelcome guests' (p.37), and she interferes with Veronica's plans by calling Ruth, the logical heir of Kuran (p.232). In the epilogue, Ruth notes that even after the house has burnt down, Mrs Griffith believes she is 'owed compensation' (p.375) for her unpaid work at Kuran. Her greed appears to reflect what John says about Veronica, that people without anything think land will change their fortunes.

Once William discovers he might inherit Kuran, John reminds him that his prospects are not yet certain. He yells at William, 'what have you been thinking? That one day I'll just hand all of this over to you, and that'll be that?' (p.137). This is ironic, considering that when he was not much older than William, John felt entitled to Kuran. Although William is set to inherit Kuran by the end of the novel, he does not share the same sense of divine entitlement. He muses that he would like to own the station and takes steps to protect John's interests, such as when he reveals that 'the bones of those people' were 'thrown in the water hole' (p.359), but his actions seem to come as much from a place of loyalty and obedience as from personal ambition.

Legacy and inheritance

Key quotes

'And when I die, I won't be leaving a hole in a cemetery or my name on a gravestone. This is what I'll be leaving.' (John, p.85)

'Discovery isn't enough. Doing something great isn't enough. Someone has to know about it, for it to mean anything. Whatever you do in this world, you have to leave someone behind who remembers.' (John, p.163)

The notions of legacy and inheritance are intertwined. Things that can be bestowed by one person can be received by another. Although several characters focus on inheriting Kuran House, only John and Ruth reflect on why people want to leave things to the next generation.

When John realises that he will not inherit Kuran, part of his desire shifts to focus on what he will leave behind. He watches Oliver Fisher squander his wealth and so, after Oliver's death, when John sells the Fisher family house and buys a farm with Harriet's inheritance, 'Oliver's legacy was complete' (p.171). John wants more for his family. Growing up on a grand station such as Kuran has instilled in him a desire to create a pastoral dynasty. John wants Ruth 'to have more, to be better than Elizabeth ever was' and he wants any potential son to grow up 'knowing without question that Kuran Station was his to inherit. Then he would look to his father with gratitude and pride, not disappointment' (p.192). His desire to leave a positive, powerful legacy is entangled with his feelings of shame about his own father's failure to do so.

One of the mistakes John makes in cultivating this legacy is failing to share his dreams with Ruth. William provides him with an opportunity to shape and groom an heir as he desires. John confesses to William, 'I have no family, no children to raise. What will happen to all this when I'm gone?' (p.109). The lure of the inheritance is tantalising to William. He reflects that his own father 'had never sat William on his knee, pointed out across the wheat fields, and promised, *One day, son, all this will be yours*' (p.111). William awakens to the possibility that Kuran might be his but fears 'his uncle might decide he was unworthy' (p.116).

As he imparts his knowledge to William, John's deeper motives unfold. Although it is clear he would like nothing more than to create a new pastoral family dynasty like the Whites, he indirectly discloses that this is because he values being remembered. He uses the artefacts belonging to explorer Alfred Kirchmeyer to impart a lesson to William: great acts alone are not enough to establish a legacy; one must 'leave someone behind who remembers' (p.163). This comment conveys the real reason John is interested in William. He wants someone who will be grateful to inherit Kuran, who will remember him and become his living embodiment.

Ruth attempts to disrupt John's attempt at creating a legacy. As she does not want, or stand to gain, Kuran after John's death, her motives for trying to talk William out of accepting his inheritance are personal. Ruth is trying to destroy John's legacy out of spite. Her hatred for her father stems from John choosing Kuran over her after she was raped; her triumph over her father would be an act of revenge. In attempting to educate William about native title, Ruth is adhering to her values. She believes that Indigenous peoples with a connection to the land should be able to make a claim on the property, or parts of the property, should the native title legislation pass. However, it is noteworthy that in the epilogue, Ruth decides 'if anyone from Cherbourg really wanted the place, they would have to lodge their claim, along with everybody else' (p.375). She disregards the fact that Kuran is not hers to give, freely or otherwise, and she becomes a defender of John's legacy.

The only inheritance bestowed in good faith is Dudley's. In a moment of clarity, he signs his farm over to John and Harriet, 'in gratitude for everything they had done. That way … he could die in peace' (p.197). Although given in good faith, his property and John's ugly court case to fight for it creates bad blood throughout the local community.

Additionally, John's use of Dudley's inheritance to build his own farming empire and eventually buy Kuran, thus estranging his wife and daughter, blemishes Dudley's good intentions.

Of course, legacy is not simply monetary or land-based. Dudley's legacy includes raping Ruth, an act that affects the rest of her life. Other characters, such as William's father, leave little in the way of legacy beyond a brief emotional impact. John's legacy, regardless of who inherits Kuran or whether it is broken up through native title claims, is the emotional and cultural disruption he causes for those around him and for the Indigenous peoples whose ancestors' bones he burnt. John imagined a grand pastoral dynasty but will instead be remembered as the man who burnt down his own house and desecrated the bodies of massacre victims.

Connection with the land

Key quotes

'Your farm was a machine, a factory to grow wheat. But this isn't anything like that. This is a piece of country. It's not just about heads of cattle per acre. This place is alive in its own right. It has a history. It's growing and changing all the time. It breathes.' (John, p.85)

'Understanding shook William. The hilltop at the campground was not a meeting place, and the stones there had no meaning. This was the only place, and his uncle had never found it.' (p.317)

John has many opinions about land in *The White Earth*. When he speaks about the land, he means more than just the property within Kuran's boundaries or the soil on which he grows wheat and runs cattle. John believes he has a special connection with the area that stems from his deep understanding of it. William comes to believe that when he had learnt 'everything about the station there was to know, he too would be ready to own it in his turn' (p.181).

John teaches William that 'you have to know where it fits in. You don't just buy a few square miles and put up a fence and say, This is it. Every stretch of earth has its own story' (p.106). He knows about the water catchment, the geography of the Darling Downs and the history of white people in the region. Put simply, John believes that 'knowledge was the essence of ownership' (p.181) but that 'possession was meaningless if it wasn't absolute' (p.192), hence his hatred for native title. He accuses William's father of not only being unknowledgeable about the land but also having 'no feeling for the country' (p.107). John uses the word 'feeling' to imply an intangible, unknowable quality, which underlies literal knowledge of the land.

What is not explored in the novel is why John finds that sharing the land renders ownership 'meaningless' (p.192). Despite his alleged spiritual connection with the land, John McIvor still sees the earth as something to have dominion over. This Judeo-Christian cultural view stems from an influential verse in the Bible:

> And God said, Let us make man in our image, after our likeness: and let them have dominion over the fish of the sea, and over the fowl of the air, and over the cattle, and over all the earth, and over every creeping thing that creepeth upon the earth. (King James Bible, Genesis 1:26)

These lines have been used over centuries to justify everything from imperialism to environmental degradation. The underlying attitude is that the planet exists for humans to use as they wish. Whether John is Christian or not does not matter, for this cultural assumption persists in the society in which he lives. It permeates the way he thinks, and he admits that he believes:

> land has to belong to someone to really come alive. It needs a human being to hear it and see it and to understand everything about it … otherwise it's just a piece of ground. (p.85)

The concept of dominion and absolute possession does not fit with sharing the land, with Indigenous peoples or otherwise, and is one of the reasons John despises Ruth's husband Carl for his socialist politics, which emphasise sharing national assets.

Indigenous characters are not present in *The White Earth* but Indigenous beliefs and John's interpretation of these beliefs are discussed. John acknowledges that Indigenous peoples can have special links with the land, but says white Australians 'can have connections with the land too, our own kind of magic. This land talks to me' (p.181). Unfortunately, what John knows and what he thinks he knows about Kuran's history are incongruous. He believes a stone circle on the hill was a gathering place for Indigenous peoples and that 'something is present on this hill. Something comes alive' (p.179). John is mistaking atmosphere and mood for spiritual significance.

John understands in an abstracted sense the Indigenous connection to the land – that Indigenous peoples have, as Queensland Museum puts it, 'a living symbiotic relationship with the land and waters of their traditional homeland estates'. But he does not grasp the care associated with native custodianship or stewardship, nor the concept of belonging to the land as if it were one's mother and a fundamental part of a person.

Towards the end of William's journey to the waterhole, the bunyip tells him that John is 'blind' (p.317) to the land and its places of power. The bunyip also says that he was dreamt 'long ago' and that 'old things still wait. In the special places' (p.316). Through this, William realises that John's connection to the land is not nearly as special as he first believed. Although William may not have spent a lifetime studying the soil through farming or logging, in that moment he understands a part of the land and its long and living history better than John could ever comprehend.

Secrets

Key quotes

'... those people are dead and gone. It's a secret now, this place.' (John, p.103)

'... the great enigma of [John's] father was suddenly laid bare. A man always so reviled, so distrusted, so dogged by whispers and frowns.' (p.349)

Secrets go hand-in-hand with lies and mystery. William's fake illness becomes a secret he is forced to keep in order to get to know John. Veronica and Doctor Moffat become his co-conspirators. The true nature of Veronica's mental illness is kept secret from William. There is an unspoken notion that such knowledge must be kept from children.

The novel is littered with secrets of small and large importance. These have a significant impact on the events in the story. To William, the forbidden upstairs of Kuran House is a mystery, kept under lock and key. John tells him 'there's nothing up here for you' (p.62) and William watches as 'day after day, the door was shut fast' (p.35), which only adds to the appeal. When William steals a set of keys and sneaks upstairs, he finds John's lovely restored bedroom and 'it was as if William had looked into his uncle's stern heart and found there something delicate and beautiful. No wonder the old man had forbidden him from the second story' (p.152). As well as this puzzling insight into his uncle, William also finds the artefacts and military uniform, wondering why the broken objects are 'kept in a fine cabinet' (p.154) and whose uniform is in the chest. The mystery of these objects is quickly dispelled as John shares their secrets with William, taking him into his confidence.

Ruth's existence is kept secret from William until later in the novel. He is unaware that he might have a competitor for his inheritance. John has explicitly stated that he has no immediate family, then explains 'there are lies and there are lies' (pp.235–6). As with the existence of the waterhole and the stone circle on the hilltop, John feels justified in lying and keeping secrets when he sees fit. It is unclear why Veronica also keeps Ruth's existence from William, but it has little bearing on the story except that it allows for Ruth to explain to William directly that she has no interest in inheriting the property.

Ruth is entangled with a darker secret, though. Her rape is not reported to the police because 'it would only shame Ruth further' (p.220). She is sent away so that knowledge of Dudley's shame is kept from everyone. The damage inflicted on her in order for John to save face stays with her and motivates her spiteful revenge later in the novel.

Several of the novel's mysteries centre on the waterhole. Initially, John tells William that the waterhole is 'a secret' (p.103) that William cannot share with his mother. This establishes a pattern of secrecy between William and his mother – he does not correct her when she thinks he ate 'a bad burger' (p.225) at the rally, for example, as he understands that his visions are only to be discussed with his uncle. Later, the waterhole becomes the source of the key secret of the story: a massacre on the land. Ruth reveals to John that Daniel McIvor covered up the massacre because it 'was a crime, it had to be kept secret' (p.358), but she is certain that 'when what your father did comes out' (p. 355), descendants of the massacre victims may be able to make a native title claim.

John reacts to this information in the only way he knows: secrecy. Even though 'the great enigma of his father was suddenly laid bare' (p.349), John wants to cover up the massacre so there is no evidence linking Indigenous peoples to the land at Kuran. He burns the bones and trusts that William will keep his secret, but his actions lead to his death. Ultimately, secrets in the narrative result in devastating revelations of the truth.

Conflicting values

Key quotes

'No one is taking one square inch of my land away. I've kept this station alive despite everything the world has thrown at me. And I did it alone.' (John, p.139)

'You know, no one really *found* Kuran. And it wasn't empty. Other people were already here.' (Ruth, p.276)

John values the land of Kuran Station, establishing a legacy and independence. Ruth, influenced by her university education and scarred by her father's rejection of her, believes that Aboriginal peoples know the land and are deserving of some land rights and compensation. She does not want to inherit Kuran for both personal and political reasons.

John made one mistake that his father didn't: he failed to communicate his wishes and dreams to his family. Daniel McIvor fosters in his son a sense of entitlement that stays with John for the rest of his life. There are several occasions when John wonders whether he should have told Harriet or Ruth about his plans to acquire Kuran Station. When he finally reveals this to Harriet, the timing is terrible. Even after they move into Kuran House, Harriet rejects John's ambitions and John himself, resulting in separation and divorce. Harriet, though very loyal, even becoming nursemaid to the man who rapes Ruth, ultimately values her relationship with her daughter above all else.

The Australian Independence League, of which John is president, comes to represent views more extreme than John's. At first it is suggested that the League is merely a reflection of John's opinions, but at the committee meeting he struggles to keep the focus on native title and has to allow a vote for a militia arm of the group. Later, after members dressed as Klansmen ruin the rally, John bids them good riddance, yet seems bitter about the experience. The extremist views of some of the radical members of the League serve to characterise John as a more reasonable, if still conservative, person.

Ruth, meanwhile, embodies a progressive way of thinking about native title. Although Ruth speaks from a position of white privilege, she is sympathetic to Indigenous land rights claims and presents William with a different side of the story than he has heard from John. She believes that Indigenous peoples deserve a chance to reclaim or at least share the land, and reflects the broad changes in Australian society's attitude that developed over the twentieth century. Scholar Elisa Bracalente notes that it is 'significant that the one who contrasts this view of land ownership is a woman' (Bracalente 2011, p.263) because it highlights the opposite attitudes and ways of thinking to the white patriarchal view John represents.

It is in Chapter 32 that the differences between John and Ruth's values become most apparent. Each time William makes a point about fixing Kuran House, about the League or about the inheritance, Ruth offers a counterpoint that makes him uncomfortable. Her presence sets the tone for the remainder of the novel. The differences in their values create tension between Ruth and John, and the rising action in the story comes to centre on who will 'win' William's loyalty and decide where John's inheritance goes. Although there are crucial differences in their beliefs and values, Ruth realises after John's death that she is like her father when she reflects on the property and notes that 'in this world, something like that wasn't just given back. It had to be fought for' (p.375).

Key point

John and Ruth symbolise two key views towards reconciliation and native title. Elisa Bracalente notes that John 'embodies the conservative landowner class and is the representative of all the discourses used to justify land dispossession through the myth of the foundation of this country' (Bracalente 2011, p.262), whereas Ruth represents a modern, more inclusive Australian attitude.

DIFFERENT INTERPRETATIONS

Different interpretations arise from different responses to a text. Over time, a text will evoke a wide range of responses from its readers, who may come from various social or cultural groups and live in very different places and historical periods. Responses by critics and reviewers can be published in newspapers, journals and books, both online and in print. They can also be expressed in discussions among readers in the media, classrooms, book groups and so on.

While there is no single correct reading or interpretation of a text, it is important to understand that an interpretation is more than a personal opinion – it is the justification of a point of view on the text. To present an interpretation of a text based on your point of view, you must use a logical argument and support it with relevant evidence from the text.

The critics' viewpoint

The reception of *The White Earth* was generally very positive. Sales and critical attention grew after the novel won the prestigious Miles Franklin Award in 2005. Critics emphasised McGahan's prose skill and use of Gothic conventions, and James Ley, a *Sydney Morning Herald* critic and later one of the last people to interview McGahan before his death, states the novel's 'symbolic vocabulary' focused around the natural elements (Ley 2004).

Several critics mention the imagery and symbolism of the man on fire. Ley calls this a 'powerful depiction of the insinuating nature of guilt', while C Max Magee, writing in American publication *The Millions*, suggests this image is 'a bit heavyhanded' (Magee 2006). Magee's American context and reduction of the novel to 'an enjoyable epic of the struggle for land Down Under' perhaps suggests a lack of the cultural understanding needed to access certain layers of meaning in the novel.

Most Australian reviews discuss the place of the novel in Australian literature favourably. Christen Cornell points out that the text does not try to speak for Aboriginal peoples (Cornell 2005) but rather, as Flora MacDonald puts it, 'joins other calls for reconciliation' (Copyright Agency n.d.) by white authors in Australian literature. The lack of Indigenous characters is revealing, as it reminds the reader of the focus on white denial and thinking (Cornell 2005).

Academic research about *The White Earth* is still emerging. Elisa Bracalente argues that McGahan does not glorify the story of Australia, but seeks to 'present the myth as constructed and deprive it of any romantic aura' (Bracalente 2011, p.239). Several stylistic choices are made to create this representation. McGahan inverts the traditional symbolism of the colour white, reversing the 'association of white with purity and positive images' (p.287), and John and Ruth are shown to represent, 'respectively, the old colonialist *terra nullius* attitude to white land ownership and the newly-negotiated, post-Mabo recognition of the rights of Indigenous Australians to land ownership' (p.261). An article in the *Griffith Review* focuses on William as a 'cipher', a 'screen onto which many vital questions can be projected – such as, for how long do we carry the sins of our ancestors?' (Griffith University 2020).

Two Interpretations of *The White Earth*

Interpretation 1: William's choices and decisions help to drive the plot.

Although he is only a child, several of William's choices lead to significant plot developments in *The White Earth*. While he hates Kuran House in his first weeks there, this hate gives way to indifference and then to admiration, until finally William can see himself as the owner of Kuran, restoring the house to its former glory, and 'in that moment, he made up his mind. He *did* want the house' (p.117). William begins to desire Kuran and makes choices to further these ambitions.

When William steals a set of keys and sneaks upstairs, he has made a decision to disobey John. Rather than getting him in trouble, his actions endear him to John, who decides to 'call it square' (p.161) in exchange for William's help with the newsletter. This also disempowers Mrs Griffith, who seems 'bereft' and in 'decline' (p.229) after her attempt to disgrace William fails. A thwarted Mrs Griffith is thus motivated to telephone Ruth.

William also chooses to wear Daniel McIvor's old Queensland Native Mounted Police hat. While it is unclear whether he does this to ingratiate himself with John or because he is intrigued by it, the hat leads to the jolly swagman sparing him in his vision, and also to the bunyip guiding him to find the bones of the massacre victims. In addition, the hat alerts Ruth to Daniel's past, and she is able to make inquiries that lead to the discovery of the massacre.

At the rally, when William decides to leave the hilltop, he triggers a vision of the man on fire. By telling John about this vision, he cultivates John's belief that he is the right person to inherit Kuran. John thinks that, due to seeing the burning man, William and he 'share the same ghosts' (p.239).

Finally, William makes critical choices that influence the plot because he chooses John over Ruth. Despite Ruth's manipulations and her shocking revelation of the massacre, William tells John about the bones in the creek bed. If William had remained quiet, he would also have remained neutral. Instead, despite feeling 'a desperate sadness' about the bones, he reveals their existence to John, adding that it was 'the things out in the hills' (p. 359) that told him where to find them. William has clearly made a decision about his loyalties, one that leads to him desecrating a grave and, finally, to his mother and uncle dying in a house fire.

Interpretation 2: William is passive, subject to the manipulations of others.

In *The White Earth*, several characters manipulate William to their own ends. Veronica keeps him home from school so he can get to know John. Although William is confused by this, Veronica does not clarify the situation and only tells him 'this is just ... an arrangement' (p.43).

By keeping William in the dark, Veronica gives him the motivation to discover their purpose in being at Kuran. Yet when William goes exploring, he gets lost and reflects that 'he hated Kuran Station, every inch of it' (p.70). He is clearly not interested in owning it.

In Chapter 15, Veronica asks William to be nice to John so that William can inherit Kuran. William says he does not know if he likes Kuran, but she tells him 'it's important that you do' (p.113). In using her status as his mother to manipulate him, Veronica pushes William into contending for John's inheritance.

An obedient child, William does what he is told, not only by Veronica but also by John. John projects complex and adult ideas onto the boy. When John yells at him for nodding in a manner John finds patronising, William begins to cry and thinks, 'he'd been doing his best, to help, to grow up. What has he done that was so wrong?' (p.139). He does not understand that no matter how well he behaves, John is going to express his anger about native title, the rally and its politics.

Later, Ruth manipulates William by trying to turn him against John. John's warning that Ruth will 'pretend to be your friend' (p.241) proves true. She informs William that 'no one really *found* Kuran. And it wasn't empty' (p.276). She creates uncertainly and confusion in William in the hope that he will reject his inheritance. When William realises this, he feels 'tricked' (p.281) but, ever passive and obedient, he obeys Ruth when she does not let him go inside and makes him listen to her talk about Aboriginal history.

William's obedience results in some dangerous situations. When John tests his loyalty by sending him to the waterhole, 'the old man's certainty blazed within' William as he departs (p.297). He does not question whether it is a good idea until he runs out of drinking water and is hoping for his mother, who does not come because John has ordered her not to search for him. Even William's visions are not something he seeks out or hopes for – they happen to him and he is the unwilling recipient. When the dead explorer speaks to him, William knows he is 'talking to the empty air' (p.310). He does not choose to talk to the bunyip, but is chosen because he bears 'the mark' (p.317). In almost all instances, William is the one who is ordered around and made to do things.

William's compliant nature results in adults using him for their own purposes. Veronica uses him to get Kuran, Ruth uses him to try to thwart John's plan, and John grooms him to become the owner he thinks Kuran needs. Although some choices are made on William's behalf because he is a child, it is clear that not all choices are made with his best interests in mind. In making these choices and decisions for him, it is the other characters, and not William, who drive events in *The White Earth*.

QUESTIONS & ANSWERS

This section focuses on your own analytical writing on the text, and gives you strategies for producing high-quality responses in your coursework and exam essays.

Essay writing – an overview

An essay on a literary work is a formal and serious piece of writing that presents your point of view on the text, usually in response to a given topic. Your 'point of view' in an essay is your interpretation of the meaning of the text's language, structure, characters, situations and events, supported by detailed analysis of textual evidence.

Analyse – don't summarise

In your essays it is important to avoid simply summarising what happens in a text.

- A **summary** is a description or paraphrase (retelling in different words) of the characters and events. For example: 'Macbeth has a horrifying vision of a dagger dripping with blood before he goes to murder King Duncan.'
- An **analysis** is an explanation of the real meaning or significance that lies 'beneath' the text's words (and images, for a film). For example: 'Macbeth's vision of a bloody dagger shows how deeply uneasy he is about the violent act he is contemplating, and conveys his sense that supernatural forces are impelling him to act.'

A limited amount of summary is sometimes necessary to let your reader know which part of the text you wish to discuss. However, always keep this to a minimum and follow it immediately with your analysis of what this part of the text is really telling us.

Plan your essay

Carefully plan your essay so that you have a clear idea of what you are going to say. The plan ensures that your ideas flow logically, that your argument remains consistent and that you stay on the topic. An essay plan should be a list of **brief dot points** covering no more than half a page.

- Include your central argument or main contention – a concise statement of your overall response to the topic.
- Write three or four dot points for each paragraph, indicating the main idea and evidence/examples from the text. Note that in your essay you will need to *expand* on these points and *analyse* the evidence.

Structure your essay

An essay is a complete, self-contained piece of writing. It has a clear beginning (the introduction), middle (several body paragraphs) and end (the last paragraph or conclusion). It must also have a central argument that runs throughout, linking each paragraph to form a coherent whole. See examples of introductions and conclusions in the 'Analysing a sample topic' and 'Sample answer' sections.

The introduction establishes your overall response to the topic. It includes your main contention and outlines the main evidence you will refer to in the course of the essay. Write your introduction *after* you have done a plan and *before* you write the rest of the essay.

The body paragraphs argue your case – they present evidence from the text and explain how this evidence supports your argument. Each body paragraph needs:

- a strong **topic sentence** (usually the first sentence) that states the main point being made in the paragraph
- **evidence** from the text, including some brief quotations
- **analysis** of the textual evidence, with **explanation** of its significance and how it supports your argument
- **links back to the topic** in one or more statements, usually towards the end of the paragraph.

Connect the body paragraphs so that your discussion flows smoothly. Use some linking words and phrases such as 'similarly' and 'on the other hand', though don't start every paragraph like this. Another strategy is to use a significant word from the last sentence of one paragraph in the first sentence of the next.

Use key terms from the topic – or synonyms for them – throughout, so the relevance of your discussion to the topic is always clear.

The conclusion ties everything together and finishes the essay. It includes strong statements that emphasise your central argument and provide a clear response to the topic.

Avoid simply restating the points made earlier in the essay – this will end on a very flat note and imply that you have run out of ideas and vocabulary. The conclusion should be a logical extension of what you have written, not just a repetition or summary of it. Writing an effective conclusion can be a challenge. Try using these tips:

- Start by linking back to the final sentence of the second-last paragraph – this helps your writing to flow, rather than leaping back to your main contention straight away.
- Use synonyms and expressions with equivalent meanings to vary your vocabulary. This allows you to reinforce your line of argument without being repetitive.
- When planning your essay, think of one or two broad statements or observations about the text's wider meaning. These should be related to the topic and your overall argument. Keep them for the conclusion, since they will give you something 'new' to say but still follow logically from your discussion. The introduction will be focused on the topic, but the conclusion can present a wider view of the text.

Essay topics

1. Analyse the impact of a relationship on William.
2. How is the reader invited to view the concept of land ownership in *The White Earth*?
3. How is the theme of inheritance explored in *The White Earth*?
4. What perspectives about possession and ownership are communicated through *The White Earth*?
5. How significant are secrets to the plot of *The White Earth*?
6. Analyse the relationship between John and Ruth.
7. "Whatever you do in this world, you have to leave someone behind who remembers." Discuss.
8. How does *The White Earth* explore the concept of entitlement?
9. "What she really wanted was for her father to be left to die alone, without anyone to follow in his footsteps, or to keep his station alive." To what extent is *The White Earth* a story about revenge and retribution?
10. How is the reader invited see *The White Earth* as a Gothic novel? How does this genre shape the text?

Vocabulary for writing on *The White Earth*

Analepsis: the literary term for flashback, in which events prior to the novel's opening are explored. They help to provide backstory and can create dramatic tension. Classic literary texts such as *Wuthering Heights* by Emily Brontë use analepsis – as does the Harry Potter series, when characters use the Pensieve to look at other characters' memories.

Australian Gothic: a subgenre of Gothic literature that focuses on the unique imagery and landscape of Australia. Examples include *Picnic at Hanging Rock* by Joan Lindsay, *The Secret River* by Kate Grenville and the film *Jindabyne*, directed by Ray Lawrence.

Bildungsroman: a novel that follows a character from youthful innocence to maturity. The term comes from the German word 'bildung', which means to educate, and 'roman', which means 'a novel'. Examples include Harper Lee's *To Kill a Mockingbird* and Charles Dickens' *Great Expectations*. *The White Earth* could arguably be labelled a bildungsroman as the events bring William from naivety to knowledge and will change the course of his future.

Character foil: a literary device whereby a character's personality is used to highlight and contrast with the personality of another character. The characters do not need to be opposites, but often have some opposing traits. Well-known examples include Macbeth and Banquo in *Macbeth*, Sherlock Holmes and Dr Watson in *A Study in Scarlet*, and Harry Potter and Neville Longbottom in *Harry Potter and the Philosopher's Stone*. In *The White Earth*, Dudley is a foil for John.

Gothic motif: a repeated pattern, image or idea in a text. It can be used to build a mood, describe a scene, carry a deeper symbolic meaning or foreshadow later events. Some classic examples of Gothic motifs include locked doors, decaying ruins, full moons and ghosts, visions and other supernatural elements. In Australian Gothic, this list can be extended to include a hostile landscape, the bush and Indigenous spiritualism.

Symbolism: a literary device that uses an object or person to represent something else for example, rope could symbolise imprisonment and birds could symbolise freedom. In *The White Earth*, McGahan uses Daniel McIvor's hat to symbolise hate and oppression of Indigenous peoples.

Imagery: rich, detailed description that appeals to the senses, particularly the visual. Like symbolism, it is an important device in Gothic texts.

Analysing a sample topic

"Whatever you do in this world, you have to leave someone behind who remembers." Discuss.

The key word in this topic is 'remembers'. It links to the theme of legacy and inheritance. The sentence quoted is said by John, so John's character and actions must form part of the response. Also interesting is the use of the world 'you'. It implies that John is instructing or directing someone – in this case, William. The use of 'you' creates an imperative, commanding tone and adds to the characterisation of John.

Quote-based questions can be as broad as this one, where you are simply asked to 'discuss' and must create your own thesis statement, or they can be followed by a more specific direction. You must develop a thesis statement that does not simply repeat the quote. If the quote relates to inheritance or legacy, then you will need to cover one or both of these themes. For instance, if you were to focus solely on legacy then you could argue that 'John McIvor's legacy is toxic', except that could leave you struggling to write to the necessary length. This wording suggests that you are going to focus on John's actual legacy, which is only touched upon in the novel's epilogue. A better thesis statement might be: 'Despite John McIvor's careful orchestration, his intended legacy of a grand multigenerational farm becomes a legacy of control, racism and desecration.'

By having a thesis statement that is detailed, but not overly complex, the essay can cover the topics in the thesis statement: that John planned his legacy, that he intended this legacy to be a farm, and that it did not eventuate as planned. This gives you more to write about and therefore scope to demonstrate an understanding of concepts, identities, events and settings in the novel.

The plan for an essay on this topic is outlined on the next four pages. This approach is only one possible way of addressing the topic.

Sample introduction

Although many people long to be remembered, few literary characters ponder this more than John McIvor in Andrew McGahan's *The White Earth*. Despite John's careful orchestration, his intended legacy of a grand multigenerational farm becomes a legacy of control, racism and desecration. John's age and failed relationship with his daughter lead to his focus on William, a distant relative who might be the one 'who remembers' John through inheriting his property. A different perspective on legacy is offered through the characterisation of the adult Ruth, who tries to ruin John's plan and heal past traumas and wrongdoings. John's actual legacy remains to be seen in the novel. He will be remembered for terrible deeds, but there is a glimmer of hope for the future in the relationship that has formed between William and Ruth.

Body paragraph outline

Paragraph 1: John's obsession with legacy must be understood in reference to his past.

- Discuss the effects of seeing the White legacy crumble. Use the quotation from the day at Kuran Station with Harriet: 'He saw the same forlorn signs of neglect' (p.145).
- Analyse the imagery of peeling paint, dead grass and rubbish, which links to Gothic motifs (which contributes to the Australian Gothic), but also links to John witnessing a (literally) crumbling legacy.
- Use the quotation about Oliver Fisher: John saw that 'Oliver's legacy was complete' (p.171). John wants more for his family and sees Oliver's legacy as too short-lived.

Paragraph 2: Although creating a powerful legacy for Ruth is what drives John, he makes a critical mistake in cultivating her as his heir.

- Introduce the idea that John's desire to leave a positive, powerful legacy is entangled with his own feelings of shame about his father.
- Use the quotation about John wanting his potential son to know 'without question that Kuran Station was his to inherit. Then he would look to his father with gratitude and pride, not disappointment' (p.192). When a son does not eventuate, John looks to Ruth.
- Highlight that although John wants Kuran to be a family farm that Ruth would inherit and 'Ruth to have more, to be better than Elizabeth ever was' (p.192), the younger Ruth is unaware of 'the whole life he'd always planned for her' (p.267).
- Analyse the divergence of values and the reasons for this. The two characters come to symbolise two different sets of values.
- Conclude with the point that the critical mistake John makes in cultivating this legacy is failing to communicate his dreams to Ruth to ensure she shares his vision and values.

Paragraph 3: William represents a second chance for John, but John establishes a rapport with William through aggressive and inappropriate methods.

- Use the quotation about John's pride being apparent when 'William could hear the pride in the way his uncle said "my land"' (p.82).
- William reflects that his own father 'had never sat William on his knee, pointed out across the wheat fields, and promised, *One day, son, all this will be yours*' (p.111). You could also use evidence relating to William awaking to the possibility that Kuran might be his (p.110) but fearing that 'his uncle might decide he was unworthy' (p.116).

- Analyse the allegorical story of explorer Alfred Kirchmeyer, which John relates to William. It is a cautionary tale, and John stresses that great acts alone are not enough to establish a legacy, that one must also 'leave someone behind who remembers' (p.163).
- Outline the dangerous situations John leads William into: William gets lost exploring the property, he is hurt at the rally, he could have died of exposure on his journey to the waterhole, and he is made to commit a crime when he collects the bones.
- Conclude with a point about an unhealthy relationship seemingly based on a blood bond but actually based on an imbalance of power.

Paragraph 4: Ruth's character serves as an obstacle to John in creating his legacy as planned.

- Introduce the concept of character as symbol. Compared with John, Ruth symbolises a different set of values and attitudes towards Indigenous peoples and land rights.
- Compare and contrast the two sets of values.
- Cite supporting evidence. When Ruth tries to open William's mind to other ways of interpreting native title and William becomes defensive, Ruth says 'that's your uncle talking' (p.284). She calls John 'another old man, clinging on to this bloody station for dear life' (p.279) and teaches William that 'other people were already here' (p.276).
- Conclude with a point about how John's lack of foresight when Ruth was a child leads to Ruth opposing him later in life.

Paragraph 5: How John is remembered will differ greatly from his intended legacy.

- Reiterate John's desire for a grand pastoral dynasty.
- Use evidence from Chapter 45, where he burns the bones.

- Use evidence from the epilogue, where Ruth decides 'if anyone from Cherbourg really wanted the place, they would have to lodge their claim, along with everybody else' (p.375). She disregards the fact that Kuran is not hers to give, freely or otherwise, yet she becomes a defender of John's legacy.
- Analyse the negative effects of John's legacy. State any potential positives.
- Conclude with a point about John being willing to create a terrible secret in order to secure the future of Kuran according to his master plan.

Sample conclusion

> How one is remembered is something that people have limited control over. Legacy can be planned and set up, but one cannot control it after death. To show its potentially negative influence, McGahan uses the character of John to demonstrate how obsession with legacy can lead to intergenerational racism and trauma. And this legacy, regardless of who inherits Kuran or whether parts are dismantled due to native title claims, is the emotional and cultural destruction wreaked on those he lived with and the Indigenous people whose ancestors' bones he burnt. John imagines a grand pastoral dynasty, yet he will be remembered as the man who burned his house down and desecrated the remains of massacre victims.

SAMPLE ANSWER

Analyse the impact of a relationship on William.

One of the central questions in Andrew McGahan's *The White Earth* is whether Ruth's influence over William will erode his loyalty to John. Throughout the second half of the novel, William finds himself caught between the opposing views of John and Ruth, both of whom hope to manipulate him in pursuit of their own agenda. Even before her arrival at Kuran Station, William is forewarned that Ruth's presence will be antagonistic: John cautions that she will be the worst of William's enemies, while Mrs Griffith relishes Ruth's impending arrival as a form of spiteful triumph over William and Veronica. Despite these cautions, Ruth nevertheless manages to exert a tremendous influence over William. By engaging with him in meaningful conversation, she distinguishes herself as the only adult to show an interest in his views, as well as his health. Ruth's relationship with William serves to highlight the toxic nature of his relationship with John.

INTRODUCTION
Introduces text and author

Foregrounds character and issue

Assumes reader has knowledge of text

Essay signposting

Like John, Ruth educates William about several topics, but while John sees William as a blank canvas on which to project his own values, Ruth adopts a more tactful approach. She arms William with the information to challenge the world views and the opinions grafted onto him by John, and ultimately reveals an underlying complexity to the issues whereas John expects dutiful parroting. This often becomes evident in their discussions regarding

BODY PARAGRAPH 1: Educating William
Compares approaches to educating William

Indigenous interests in land. John tells William that the Darling Downs were empty grasslands, but Ruth says that 'other people were already here' and they founded the grasslands for which the Darling Downs are famous. Similarly, she calls William out on the way he reacts to discussing Indigenous peoples, noting that his opinions sound like John's rather than his own. Ruth symbolises a set of values and beliefs to which William has never been exposed, and she seemingly seeks to empower William rather than demanding obedience from him. She is, however, a complex character, and the warnings foreshadowing her arrival prove to have some substance.

Direct evidence

Symbolism

Connecting sentence

BODY PARAGRAPH 2: Ruth's agenda

Topic sentence

Foreshadowing

Connects to themes such as legacy

Impact on reader

Impact on plot

From the moment she arrives at Kuran, there is little doubt that Ruth has her own agenda, and this compromises her interactions with William. The more spiteful elements of her character are foreshadowed during her vandalism of the cemetery's crumbling angel, where her disregard for both the symbolic protector of the White family legacy and John's property is telling. In Chapter 32, Ruth shares information about her life, including that her mother left John and 'had to take him to court in the end'. The reader knows she is only revealing these details to portray John negatively, and soon William realises this too. Ruth also uses the information gleaned from conversations with William as ammunition for her vengeful undertaking against John – for example, when William unwittingly reveals that Kuran is held as a perpetual lease, and when she discovers that Daniel McIvor was responsible for leading a massacre of Indigenous people at the waterhole. Her discovery unfortunately leads to John desecrating the bones of the victims in order to hide proof of the massacre. Ruth is a complex character in that her values and beliefs represent a sympathetic and empowering view of Indigenous peoples and land rights, yet her deceptions mean she is not an entirely likeable character.

Linking sentence

Despite some unpleasant character traits, Ruth looks after William in a way no other character does, even when Kuran Station is no longer at stake. In the epilogue, Ruth keeps 'the long vigil of the night' over William's bed, showing that she will not abandon William to grow up without a familiar figure in his life. The reader is left with hope that Ruth will stay by William's side, no matter how it complicates the inheritance. Even more importantly, Ruth is the only person to search for William during his journey to the waterhole. Unlike his own mother, who is under John's sway, Ruth is compelled only by her concern and goes looking for William 'as soon as she heard. And then again this morning'. Ruth could have let William die, making her revenge on John easier, but she chose not to because she exhibits the inherent human desire to protect children.

BODY PARAGRAPH 3: Positive traits

Topic sentence

Direct evidence

Impact on reader

Direct evidence

While her influence is not as formative as John's, Ruth plays an important role in shaping William in the second half of *The White Earth*. Although she is successful in interrupting John's plans and in making William reflect on John's opinions, she is not wholly successful in undermining William's loyalty to John. Ruth's key roles in the second half of the novel are to serve as a source of dramatic tension and to symbolise a belief in land rights. Ruth's agenda is arguably nobler than John's, but could result in fewer material gains for William and herself.

CONCLUSION

Reiterates thesis statement

REFERENCES & READING

Text

McGahan, A 2004, *The White Earth*, Allen & Unwin, Sydney.

Other references

Australian Institute of Aboriginal and Torres Strait Islander Studies 2019, 'Mabo Case', 31 May, https://aiatsis.gov.au/explore/articles/mabo-case

Bracalente, E 2011, 'In the Shadow of the Australian Legend: Re-reading Australian Literature', PhD thesis, Murdoch University.

Carr-Boyd, W 1908, 'The Mount Ida Blacks', *The West Australian*, 14 December, https://trove.nla.gov.au/newspaper/article/26216046

Copyright Agency n.d., '*The White Earth*', https://readingaustralia.com.au/books/the-white-earth/

Cornell, C 2005, 'Repressed History Book Review', *Cultural Studies Review*, vol. 11, no. 2, pp. 213–17.

Griffith University 2020, 'On *The White Earth*, by Andrew McGahan', *Griffith Review*, vol. 69, April, https://www.griffithreview.

Kill Your Darlings 2012, 'Conversation with Andrew McGahan', 9 July, https://www.killyourdarlings.com.au/article/in-conversation-andrew-mcg/

Ley, J 2004, '*The White Earth*', *The Sydney Morning Herald*, 1 May, https://www.smh.com.au/entertainment/books/the-white-earth-20040501-gdiu70.html

Magee, C M 2006, '*The White Earth* by Andrew McGahan: A Review', *The Millions*, 23 January, https://themillions.com/2006/01/white-earth-by-andrew-mcgahan-review.html

Publishers Weekly 2005, 'Fiction Book Review: *The White Earth* by Andrew McGahan', 19 September, https://www.publishersweekly.com/978-1-56947-417-4

Southern Poverty Law Center 2015, 'Active Ku Klux Klan Groups', 3 March, https://www.splcenter.org/fighting-hate/intelligence-report/2015/active-ku-klux-klan-groupscom/24754/